SpringerBriefs in Applied Sciences and Technology

Safety Management

Series Editors

Eric Marsden, FonCSI, Toulouse, France

Caroline Kamaté, FonCSI, Toulouse, France

Jean Pariès, FonCSI-ICSI, Toulouse, France

The SpringerBriefs in Safety Management present cutting-edge research results on the management of technological risks and decision-making in high-stakes settings.

Decision-making in high-hazard environments is often affected by uncertainty and ambiguity; it is characterized by trade-offs between multiple, competing objectives. Managers and regulators need conceptual tools to help them develop risk management strategies, establish appropriate compromises and justify their decisions in such ambiguous settings. This series weaves together insights from multiple scientific disciplines that shed light on these problems, including organization studies, psychology, sociology, economics, law and engineering. It explores novel topics related to safety management, anticipating operational challenges in high-hazard industries and the societal concerns associated with these activities.

These publications are by and for academics and practitioners (industry, regulators) in safety management and risk research. Relevant industry sectors include nuclear, offshore oil and gas, chemicals processing, aviation, railways, construction and healthcare. Some emphasis is placed on explaining concepts to a non-specialized audience, and the shorter format ensures a concentrated approach to the topics treated.

The SpringerBriefs in Safety Management series is coordinated by the Foundation for an Industrial Safety Culture (FonCSI), a public-interest research foundation based in Toulouse, France. The FonCSI funds research on industrial safety and the management of technological risks, identifies and highlights new ideas and innovative practices, and disseminates research results to all interested parties. For more information: https://www.foncsi.org/

Hervé Laroche · Corinne Bieder ·
Jesús Villena-López
Editors

Managing Future Challenges for Safety

Demographic Change, Digitalisation and Complexity in the 2030s

Editors
Hervé Laroche
ESCP Business School
Paris, France

Corinne Bieder
Ecole nationale de l'aviation civile
University of Toulouse
Toulouse, France

Jesús Villena-López
Ergotec
Madrid, Spain

This work was supported by Foundation for an Industrial Safety Culture

ISSN 2191-530X ISSN 2191-5318 (electronic)
SpringerBriefs in Applied Sciences and Technology
ISSN 2520-8004 ISSN 2520-8012 (electronic)
SpringerBriefs in Safety Management
ISBN 978-3-031-07804-0 ISBN 978-3-031-07805-7 (eBook)
https://doi.org/10.1007/978-3-031-07805-7

© The Editor(s) (if applicable) and The Author(s) 2022. This book is an open access publication.
Open Access This book is licensed under the terms of the Creative Commons Attribution 4.0 International License (http://creativecommons.org/licenses/by/4.0/), which permits use, sharing, adaptation, distribution and reproduction in any medium or format, as long as you give appropriate credit to the original author(s) and the source, provide a link to the Creative Commons license and indicate if changes were made.
The images or other third party material in this book are included in the book's Creative Commons license, unless indicated otherwise in a credit line to the material. If material is not included in the book's Creative Commons license and your intended use is not permitted by statutory regulation or exceeds the permitted use, you will need to obtain permission directly from the copyright holder.
The use of general descriptive names, registered names, trademarks, service marks, etc. in this publication does not imply, even in the absence of a specific statement, that such names are exempt from the relevant protective laws and regulations and therefore free for general use.
The publisher, the authors, and the editors are safe to assume that the advice and information in this book are believed to be true and accurate at the date of publication. Neither the publisher nor the authors or the editors give a warranty, expressed or implied, with respect to the material contained herein or for any errors or omissions that may have been made. The publisher remains neutral with regard to jurisdictional claims in published maps and institutional affiliations.

This Springer imprint is published by the registered company Springer Nature Switzerland AG
The registered company address is: Gewerbestrasse 11, 6330 Cham, Switzerland

Series Editor's Foreword

Anticipating the 'industry of the future', the impact that the evolution of society, technologies, organisation and communication modes have on human work and modes of production, is a priority for the Foundation for an Industrial Safety Culture (FonCSI) and its partners.

What will be at stake for industrial safety in complex high-hazard industrial systems in 2030/40? How will the contribution of human operators to safety evolve? Can we speculate on the role of and relationships between industry, regulators and other stakeholders and their impact on safety over this timeframe?

This collective volume is the fruit of a 'strategic analysis'—a research methodology developed by FonCSI that brings together academics and practitioners for inquiry, debate and anticipation—aimed at addressing these issues. The book presents the contributions of international experts who were invited to explain and confront their viewpoints during a two-day digital seminar held in November 2020 and which was the highlight of the strategic analysis. The book focuses on safety in high-hazard industry sectors such as oil and gas, energy and transportation, but does not hesitate to draw inspiration from other areas such as the military or medical and digital services, with a view to offering some food for thought and ways forward to face the challenges of a rapidly changing world.

December 2021

Caroline Kamaté
FonCSI
Toulouse, France

Contents

1 **Times Are Changing and so Is Safety** 1
   Corinne Bieder and Jesús Villena-López
   1.1 Safety Today: A Dominant Model 1
        1.1.1 Main Characteristics of the Dominant
               Safety Model in High-Risk Industries Seen
               from a Distance: Formal Similarities 2
        1.1.2 A Closer Look at the Dominant Safety Model
               in High-Risk Industries: Some Nuances 3
        1.1.3 From a Demo Version Based on Risk Control
               to Real Versions also Calling on Adaptation 4
   1.2 Why Should We Think About Safety Differently
        in the Future? 4
        1.2.1 Technological Evolution, Especially Massive
               Digitalisation in Many Areas 5
        1.2.2 Socioeconomic and Industrial Evolution 7
        1.2.3 Societal and Sociopolitical Evolution 9
   1.3 Could the Models of Safety as Demonstrated
        and as Practised Converge? 10
   1.4 Book Outline 10
   References 12

2 **Evolution in the Way of Waging War for Combatants
   and Military Leaders** 13
   Gérard de Boisboissel
   2.1 Introduction 13
   2.2 Foreseen Changes in the Way of Conducting War 14
        2.2.1 Displacement of the Combatant's Action 14
        2.2.2 A New Threat: Access to Innovation by Enemies 15
        2.2.3 How to Avoid Dissemination? 15

	2.3	Impact on Responsibilities	15
		2.3.1 Changes at the Organisational Level	15
		2.3.2 Still the Need for Human Responsibility When Using the Machine	16
		2.3.3 Responsibility is also Common to All Stakeholders	16
	2.4	The Place of Leaders in Complex Systems	17
		2.4.1 Leaders Must Always Control the Use of an Autonomous System	17
		2.4.2 Operators Must Have Confidence When Delegating Tasks to an Autonomous System	18
		2.4.3 Cognitive Overload: The Need for a Digital Assistant	18
		2.4.4 AI Will Influence the Decisions Made by the Leader	19
	2.5	New Rules for Autonomous Systems	19
		2.5.1 Machines Have to Respect Law Rules	19
		2.5.2 Hardware and Components Should Be Protected by Design	20
	2.6	Towards an International Standardisation	21
		2.6.1 Civilian Level	22
		2.6.2 Military Level	22
		2.6.3 Lethal Autonomous Weapon Systems	22
	2.7	Conclusion	23
	References		23
3	**Learning from the Military**		25
	Hervé Laroche and Florence Reuzeau		
	3.1	Introduction	25
	3.2	Six Key Points	26
		3.2.1 Inevitability	26
		3.2.2 Responsibility and Control	26
		3.2.3 Trustability	27
		3.2.4 Self-Learning Machines and Human Training	28
		3.2.5 Cognitive Overload	28
		3.2.6 Empowerment Paradox	29
	3.3	Final Comments	30
	References		31
4	**Critical Digital Services**		33
	John Allspaw		
	4.1	Introduction	33
	4.2	Growing Criticality	34
	4.3	Growing Consequences	35
	4.4	The Landscape of Roles and Skills	35
	4.5	What Does the Future of Work in CDS Look Like?	36
	4.6	What Can Industry Adaptation to COVID-19 Tell Us?	37

	4.7	A Critical yet Nascent Domain	38
		4.7.1 Challenges	38
		4.7.2 Opportunities and Advantages for Researchers	38
	References		39

5 Between Natural and Artificial Intelligence 41
Stian Antonsen
    5.1 Introduction 41
    5.2 The Changing Nature of Work 42
    5.3 Uncertainty and Epistemic Accidents 43
    5.4 Assumptions and Uncertainty in Artificial Intelligence 44
    5.5 The Human Contribution to Safety in Future 46
    5.6 Implications—The Future of Risk 48
    References 49

6 Careers Surpassing a Half-Century: A Look at Japan and France 51
Akira Tose and Dounia Tazi
    6.1 The Situation in Japan: A Possible Projection of What the Future Situation Will Be in Europe and France 51
    6.2 Careers Surpassing a Half-Century: The Main Challenges .. 52
    6.3 What Strategies Can Be Used to Manage This Situation? A Few Examples Being Tested in Japan 53
        6.3.1 Giving Employees the Possibility of Updating Their Skills and Knowledge Throughout Their Career 53
        6.3.2 Managing the Mix of Generations 54
        6.3.3 Offering Rewarding Positions to the Most Experienced 54
        6.3.4 Ergonomics and Consideration of Human and Organisational Factors 55
    6.4 Discussion 55
        6.4.1 Age Limit and Safety 56
        6.4.2 Generational Mix and Safety 56
    References 57

7 Senior Mentoring, Skills Transfer Subject to Conditions 59
Tania Navarro Rodríguez and Alexandre Largier
    7.1 Introduction 59
    7.2 Mentoring, Numerous Forms and Varied Contexts 60
    7.3 Seniors, All Mentors 61
    References 62

8 Airbus Global Workforce Forecast (GWF) 63
Béatrice Pons, Jean-Hugues Rodriguez, and Florence Reuzeau
    8.1 Introduction 63
    8.2 Involve Everyone in the Transformation of the Company .. 64

	8.3	Deep and Fast Transformation: A Shared Concern	64
	8.4	The Airbus Competence Strategy: A Full Engagement with International Organisations	65
	8.5	Conclusion	66

9 **Rethinking Competencies in Hazardous Industries** 67
Alexandre Largier
   9.1   Introduction: Why Study Competencies in the Nuclear Industry? 67
   9.2   Limitations of Managerial Approach to Competencies 68
   9.3   Rethinking Competencies in Work Activities 70
        9.3.1   Analysing the Situational Implementation of Competencies 70
        9.3.2   Importance of Organisational Dimensions in the Implementation of Competencies 71
   9.4   Conclusion 72
   References 73

10 **The Design of "Future Work" in Industrial Contexts** 75
Flore Barcellini
   10.1   Introduction 75
   10.2   Lessons Learned for Worker–Technology Cooperation Research and Project Design Management 76
        10.2.1   Is Worker–Technology Cooperation a Myth or a Possible Reality? 76
        10.2.2   A Lack of a Participative and Work-Centred Project Management Approach in Introducing Cooperative Technology at Work 77
   10.3   So, Are Ongoing Transformations of Work in Relation to Technology Neglecting Lessons Learned from the Past? 78
        10.3.1   A Strong Techno-Determinism, a Lack of Explainability and an Under-Estimation of the Socio-organisational Impacts of Technologies 78
        10.3.2   A Claim for More Participative and Collaborative Project Management with a Lack of Operational Proposals 80
   10.4   What Recommendations to Foster the Success of Projects in Terms of Health, Safety and Performance? 80
   References 81

11 **Standardization and Risk Regulation for High-Hazard Industries** 85
Michael Baram and Corinne Bieder
   11.1   Introduction 85
   11.2   Interplay Between Standards and Risk Regulation 86

		11.3	Toward a Better Understanding of Standardization	88
		11.4	Standardization and AI	90
		11.5	A Concerning Trend in Progress	91
		References		92
12	Adaptive Imagination at Work in Health Care			95
	Steven Shorrock			
		12.1	Introduction	95
		12.2	Responding to a Rapidly Changing World	96
		12.3	Work-as-Imagined and Work-as-Done	98
		12.4	Human-Centred Design and Systems Thinking and Practice	101
		12.5	Leadership and Social Capital	102
		12.6	Lessons for Future Work	103
		References		103
13	Conjectures and Challenges of Safety Management			105
	Jean Pariès			
		13.1	Changes in the World and Changes in the Minds	105
		13.2	The Future of the 'Compliant yet Intelligent Operator' Injunction	107
		13.3	Rise and Fall of a Paradigm Shift	108
		13.4	The Risk of a Late and Stale Evolution of Safety Management	110

Chapter 1
Times Are Changing and so Is Safety

Corinne Bieder and Jesús Villena-López

Abstract Reflecting about the challenges ahead and the evolution of safety raises a multitude of questions about the future but also about safety. This introductory chapter first nuances the notion of safety as if it were a homogeneous whole. It starts with an overview of the macro-safety model that underpins safety in high-risk industries, or more precisely, of the way industries are expected by society, and thus regulators, to ensure the safety of their operations. Following this safety "as demonstrated" view, it zooms in closer to the field and underlines some discrepancies between this "control" perspective and the actual practices contributing to the safety of high-risk industries, including non-proceduralised ones. It then explores some of the major evolution trends for 2040 and the uncertainties attached to them and reflects upon their possible effects on safety models in the future. With this global picture in mind illustrating the complexity of the topic addressed by the book, the last section provides an overview of the content of the book and its various constitutive chapters.

Keywords Safety · Safety management · Safety model · Future · High risk · Evolution · Digitalisation

1.1 Safety Today: A Dominant Model

Describing how safety works in high-risk industries, and more specifically the role played by humans at individual, organisational or even societal levels can be done in different ways depending on the level of detail and specificity one decides to adopt. From a very global perspective, one could say that the "visible" safety frameworks in high-risk industries share similar characteristics. Yet, when going into further detail,

C. Bieder (✉)
ENAC, University of Toulouse, Toulouse, France
e-mail: corinne.bieder@enac.fr

J. Villena-López
Ergotec, Madrid, Spain

closer to the field and real practices, one needs to introduce some nuances to the macro-"exhibited" model of how safety is ensured.

This section starts with an overview of the macro-safety model that underpins safety in high-risk industries, or more precisely, the way industries are expected by society, and thus regulators, to ensure the safety of their operations. It summarises the main characteristics of this global safety "as demonstrated" view. It then zooms in closer to the field and underlines some discrepancies between this "control" perspective and the actual practices contributing to the safety of high-risk industries, including non-proceduralised ones.

1.1.1 Main Characteristics of the Dominant Safety Model in High-Risk Industries Seen from a Distance: Formal Similarities

Historically in high-risk industries, the dominant safety model in terms of the role of humans has been based on the compliance with rules, processes and procedures at all levels, from governments through laws, to first-line operators through detailed procedures [7]. Hazardous industries are highly regulated from the outside with safety authorities developing regulatory material and ensuring oversight. This approach reflects the societal expectations of total control and clear responsibilities for the safety of new technologies with high damage potential, through the reduction, if not elimination, of uncertainties. For similar reasons, high-risk organisations are also highly proceduralised from the inside with organisational processes and procedures to standardise practices at all levels and avoid variability.

Anticipating everything, developing a priori safe responses and expecting humans to implement them is the driving force of safety as imagined and demonstrated. The underlying philosophy is to reduce uncertainty to almost zero and control risks. In such perspective, uncertainty comes down to epistemic uncertainty. Any unanticipated situation is explained through a shortfall in the risk model which is completed after the facts and still believed complete (or complete enough).

Since the 1990s, Safety Management Systems have been progressively adopted in many high-risk industries with the ambition to move away from a compliance-based to a performance-based approach to safety, whereby experience is used as a feedback loop to improve risk models, and organisations have more leeway regarding the risk reduction measures and are able to identify those best suited to their specific characteristics. This evolution involves a clear definition of safety accountabilities. A major characteristic of safety management in high-risk industries has always been that it ought to be auditable (whether from the outside, the inside or both) and accountabilities should be easy to establish.

This change of scale from a regulatory authority defining all the standards to be complied with to organisations taking a more important role in it and integrating the lessons from experience remains in line with the foundations of the previous approach and societal expectations about the safety of high-risk industries.[1] Overall, the safety model is still based on the belief that uncertainty can be reduced to almost nothing if not completely eliminated and that safety can be totally controlled this way. In such a framework, the role of humans is preconditioned.

1.1.2 A Closer Look at the Dominant Safety Model in High-Risk Industries: Some Nuances

Although this global framework of safety as imagined and as demonstrated has its own internal consistency, practices are not fully in line with it as already extensively documented in the scientific literature.

Within industries, although most of them rely on SMSs, the content and what it corresponds to varies significantly from one organisation to another, as does the credit they accord the usefulness of the SMS. Practices in terms of SMS implementation vary from mere compliance with the SMS regulation seen as paperwork to an actual reflexive activity of how to enhance the way safety is managed that most often also entails other activities beyond the SMS itself [3, 4].

In the first case, safety is managed through the demonstration model only with clear accountabilities, roles and procedures supposed to be sufficient to control risks. A number of high-risk organisations turned to consultants to develop their formal SMS, due to a lack of internal competent resources, thereby opting for another source of standardisation, that of the consulting company [1].

In the second case, organisations acknowledge the inevitable existence of contingencies and develop other means beyond risk control to cope with real situation uncertainties, such as resilience capabilities. However, in parallel, they need to maintain a formal demonstration that everything has been put in place to manage safety according to the auditable SMS requirements. Therefore, two worlds coexist within advanced organisations: (a) a formal safety management one used to provide external demonstration that safety is under control and (b) other safety enhancement strategies supporting a world of practices described in the scientific literature showing for example that: there is more to first-line operator activity than a mere implementation of procedures; operational managers rely on a combination of practices beyond formal processes to actually contribute to safety [2, 8].

Even at the safety governance level, where the formal model as imagined and asserted involves a clear boundary and separation of roles between authorities and industrial organisations, practices are more complex. In order to compensate for the lack of qualitative and quantitative internal resources, regulatory and oversight

---

[1] There are some exceptions to this, although it is by far the dominant model, such as, for example, the oil and gas industry in Norway, where the relationship between the regulatory authority and the industry is collaborative [5].

authorities sometimes involve big industrial companies in the development of regulations and acceptable means of compliance that then serve as a basis for the entire industry.

1.1.3 From a Demo Version Based on Risk Control to Real Versions also Calling on Adaptation

Although the social control of risks in high-risk industries still relies on a formal model of risk control where uncertainty is reduced to almost nothing, practices differ to some extent from this external demonstration framework to actually cope with the inevitable contingencies of the real situations faced at all levels, from first-line operators to higher managerial levels. Yet, some of these practices escape some of the key foundations of today's social control, especially (almost) total control, auditability, accountability. To what extent will these foundations be challenged or reinforced in the future, and thus possibly affect safety models (either formal or practised or both) and more specifically the role played by humans in the safety of high-risk industries?

1.2 Why Should We Think About Safety Differently in the Future?

Although so far, the evidence of the limitations of the "as demonstrated" safety model has translated into the development of dissonant parallel practices, some major trends are foreseeable in the future in many areas. This section explores some of these trends, especially the technological evolution, the socioeconomic and industrial evolution and the societal and sociopolitical evolution. For each of them, it:

- briefly describes the main trends, from the ones already underway to more uncertain or speculative ones;
- analyses the challenges or opportunities they already represent for existing safety models, either "as demonstrated" or as practised;
- discusses how they could possibly further destabilise or reinforce the current models in the future.

With all the humility that is necessary in such an endeavour, the following subsections address the aforementioned three main areas of evolution and their possible impact on safety models. The trends are addressed independently from one another for the sake of readability, hardly ever touching upon their links. Yet, they are interrelated with one another, with possible emergences that cannot be anticipated.

1.2.1 Technological Evolution, Especially Massive Digitalisation in Many Areas

The digital revolution is already underway in many areas of our personal and professional lives. More and more data are collected in more and more domains, with increasing capabilities to process them and to cross-reference different sources and types of data. The reign of artificial intelligence (AI) is proclaimed for tomorrow if not today with huge impacts announced in many fields. This trend, although massive, is to be nuanced in practice though when considering the scope of applicability of AI.

Nevertheless, several changes at several levels likely to affect safety are made possible by this technological leap. For example, at management level, the boundaries between domains (e.g. production, maintenance and safety) or between professional and personal worlds could be blurred by the crossing of data from different sources. At a more operational level, new technologies (AI) are already leading to new systems and forms of interactions. Although their use in high-risk organisations is still limited, especially for safety critical functions, they could further develop in the future in these areas as well. If we broaden the picture, old and advanced technologies will coexist in work situations or at least in organisations. This situation is not unknown and already started with automation decades ago, but the trend seems to be accelerating and generalising. In this landscape, an evolution of jobs and required competencies is anticipated, even though real figures are for the time being still lower than the storytelling around AI is suggesting [9].

At a wider societal scale, authors like Matyjasik and Guenoun [6] envisage a possible shift from today's governance regime to other regimes enabled or fostered by these new possibilities, even though the symptoms of such evolution remain timid today.

1.2.1.1 Main Challenges Faced by the Current Model in the Face of this Technological Evolution

The massive use of digital technology has already started to challenge the dominant safety model in several respects.

One of the areas most challenged by artificial intelligence is the certification of technology. In the "safety as demonstrated" model, certification plays a major role, whereby a new technology is considered safe from a priori safety analyses, even though they are refined and completed through experience. Certification of technology is currently based on the assumption that the technology behaves as it did at the time of certification. This assumption can no longer be made with AI and its evolving performance by design.

The massive digitalisation trend also leads to an increasing exposure to cyber-threats, some of which are possibly affecting safety. This calls for considering safety and security as intertwined, although they have historically been addressed separately from one another and still are today in terms of both governance, management, methods and research.

1.2.1.2 Other Possible Technology-Related Sources of Destabilisation of the Current Dominant Safety Model

Beyond the challenges that the current safety model is already facing, other aspects of the massive digitalisation trend may contribute to changing the safety management landscape in the future, although with great caution from the authors considering the level of uncertainty.

The increasing use of and value attached to data may create an imbalance between those who have the data and the capabilities including competencies to process them and those who do not. This may lead to new roles between safety regulators and industrials. Indeed, the data regarding operations are mainly gathered by the industrial partners themselves and the capabilities to process them are currently developed internally as well to support the overall organisational performance. An increased reliance on data to support safety management and safety governance puts safety authorities in a position where access to data and associated competences to process them needs to be negotiated with industrial companies.

The current governance approach could be even more destabilised if, pushed by new technological capabilities, authorities actually stop working in silos. This would lead to an evolution of structures and means of oversight, and possibly, as envisaged by Matyjasik and Guenoun [6], to an evolution of the actors of governance.

The uncertainty is huge as to whether the importance given to data will continue to grow or the use of data will be framed one way or another in the future. Even though one can only speculate at this stage, the massive use of data raises some additional questions as to how it could interplay with safety in the future, such as: could it possibly lead to the merging of data gathered in the professional scope and personal data gathered outside? Could safety monitoring use personal data on top of professional information?

Regarding the possible influence of digitalisation on the philosophy of the current dominant safety model, views diverge. Some believe that massive digitalisation can increase the power to anticipate (e.g. through numerical twins) and thus further reduce uncertainty, which would reinforce the historical philosophy of safety. Others believe on the contrary that the massive digitalisation will increase uncertainty, and thus the possibility to be surprised (a kind of new normal digital accidents). This rather calls for a different role of humans in the safety of high-risk industries, closer to that observed in practice but not officially and socially acknowledged. Whether it would change the view on social control of risk is still an open question.

1.2.2 Socioeconomic and Industrial Evolution

Beyond technologies, other evolutions are ongoing or foreseen in the socioeconomic and industrial areas.

Demographics is one of the less uncertain trends. Crossed with the socioeconomic dimension, it may lead to the ageing of professional staff, as has already started in Japan for example. This means a wide span of ages, each with their own competencies, motivations and perspectives, working in the same company and sometimes together.

Regarding industry, the trend that started in the 1980s with the emergence of fragmented and interconnected organisations continues to develop at an international scale, including in high-risk industries. It means that several sites, countries and nationalities are involved in making the organisation work. Although this trend is not new per se, what might change in the future is the distribution of activities across countries. Whereas major international corporations used to be led by western countries, the distribution of industrial power has started to evolve. The COVID-19 pandemic might have led some countries to considering the relocation of some industries to Europe, for example, but whether this inclination will actually turn into fact is still uncertain.

What seems to be increasing is the power of the major economic actors, especially compared to that of national states and their regulatory authorities. This phenomenon leads in some cases to what some authors call the capture of regulatory authorities, for example through an influence on the recruitment of authorities' staff, and thus challenges the independence of authorities, one of the current pillars of safety governance.

In the socioeconomic area, an "uberisation" trend of the economy and labour relationships has already started in some countries, with massive externalisation and subcontracting. This evolution leads to more imbalance between employers and employees through the weakening of unions and an increased power of professional elitism in the hands of the happy few in a context of scarce employment. To what extent could this trend be generalised at the international scale remains an open question.

1.2.2.1 Main Challenges Faced by the Current Model in the Face of this Socioeconomic and Industrial Evolution

The socioeconomic and industrial evolution reinforces and complicates some questions that have been around for a while, especially among academics but that the dominant model managed to escape so far. However, by making some challenges more obvious and salient, it could reach a point where even the dominant model would be destabilised.

The acceleration and generalisation of fragmentation and interconnection of organisations as well as subcontracting and externalisation challenges the development of safety culture. Safety culture is needed not only within organisations, but also across organisations that have different objectives in a context where the sense of belonging to an organisation, or even to an industry, is low and the labour relationships decline including as far as safety is concerned. The ageing of professional staff may add to this diversity of profiles having to work together, and thus to the challenge of developing or maintaining a safety culture. Although safety culture is not always directly or clearly part of the dominant model in the sense of a dedicated regulation and oversight of this aspect, at least the narrative around safety culture might have to be reconsidered.

Another direct challenge to the dominant model is posed by the socioeconomic and industrial evolution: the one-size-fits-all requirements (whether regulatory or internal) and safety management model focused on individual organisations. With the evolution underway and accelerating, the very notion of organisation is destabilised. Furthermore, these requirements are increasingly recognised, including within big international industrial companies, as not being applicable everywhere since they are decontextualised.

1.2.2.2 Possible Other Sources of Destabilisation Related to Socioeconomic and Industrial Evolution of the Current Dominant Safety Model

Today, the regulatory requirements are developed by major Western industrial actors supporting regulatory authorities, and then imposed on the industry as a whole, that is across organisations of different sizes and natures and across the world for internationally "regulated" industries such as aviation. Although, there is currently some interest for both major industrials and regulators in this approach, at least around the "safety as demonstrated" model, the main influencers could change in the future with major industrials possibly changing hands and continents (e.g. from Europe or North America to Asia) and regulators from non-western countries becoming more influential. Would new standards be developed? Would the whole model of regulation and oversight as it exists today be revisited? If yes, to what extent? Would high-risk industrial companies decide to install their headquarters in countries where safety regulations are less stringent? Would they rather intervene in the recruitment of regulatory staff and control it to a certain extent, thereby challenging one of the key conditions of the safety as demonstrated model, that is the independence of authorities? Although uncertain, these possible evolutions could destabilise not only the predominance of western standards, but also possibly the safety governance regimes and the "safety as demonstrated" model that so far has provided a kind of illusion of control that still seems socially acceptable, that is sufficiently reassuring at least in appearance to all safety stakeholders (see Fukushima).

1.2.3 Societal and Sociopolitical Evolution

Some trends are also observed at the societal and sociopolitical levels that could also impact existing safety models. For example, although trust in public services was already challenged in the 1980s, the scientific controversies around climate change or even more recently COVID-19 seem to have further increased the distrust towards experts and institutions. At the same time, an increasing attention is paid, including by civil society, to concerns like climate change or health care. In some cases, this attention also translates into a growing involvement of civil society (or a desire to be involved) in the governance of topics citizens feel concerned with.

All this is happening in a context where access to data and information (whether validated or not) is much easier and faster than it used to be. Today's communication environment (e.g. social media) enables a fast and broad dissemination of information, and thus societal mobilisation.

On another note, with the COVID-19 crisis, the interrelations between various stakes (e.g. health, economic, social) have been extensively illustrated. Although this is neither new nor limited to healthcare crises, the acknowledgement that multiple stakes coexist at the same time (likewise, high-risk industry means employment, economic activity, etc., at the same time as safety) may become more explicit and challenge the current model of governance, especially that submitted to external demonstration, addressing each stake individually.

1.2.3.1 Main Challenges Faced by the Current Model in the Face of this Societal Evolution

The current safety governance model involving industrials and regulators, who are supposedly independent and representing the voice of the public, was challenged in several cases such as following the Fukushima nuclear accident or more recently the Boeing 737 MAX crashes. In the latter case, the investigation explicitly and publicly pointed out the lack of independence of the US Federal Aviation Administration in its oversight duty. Although it is not the first case where blurred relationships between industrials and regulators were highlighted, the current information and societal environment might amplify the impact on the social acceptability of the current governance model from which civil society as such is absent.

1.2.3.2 Possible Other Sources of Destabilisation Related to Societal Evolution of the Current Dominant Safety Model

More generally, building on what happened with climate change, where the societal pressure increased to a point where it pushed the political sphere to evolve and take this societal concern more seriously than before, one could anticipate an evolution of the current safety governance model, and thus of the "safety as demonstrated" model.

Whereas today, this model mainly involves industrial companies and regulators, the increasing external scrutiny carried out by civil society could turn into more acknowledged and formal roles in the future.

In this power game, the control of information becomes crucial. Combined with the digitalisation mentioned earlier, the forces might be imbalanced between the industry collecting more and more data and regulators and the civil society possibly more dependent upon the data and their processing, and thus interpretation.

Furthermore, in times of growing public interest in health and climate change issues, the importance given by the public society to safety could evolve and a new hierarchy emerge among all these aspects.

1.3 Could the Models of Safety as Demonstrated and as Practised Converge?

Overall, the identified trends could destabilise in several ways the current dual approach to safety, where the model of safety as demonstrated and as practised coexist although they are widely acknowledged to be different. Whether the challenges and opportunities these trends represent will increase the gap between the two, possibly up to a crisis of the "safety as demonstrated" model, or will conversely reduce the gap, cannot be predicted. Yet, from different angles, both new societal expectations and new tool capabilities are likely to drive changes in the way safety is managed in the future.

1.4 Book Outline

The following chapters expand on some of the evolutions mentioned above. Although not addressing all of them, they provide different perspectives on some of the major changes likely to impact not only safety as demonstrated but also safety as practised.

It first explores the issue of digitalisation and the many challenges it involves.

In Chap. 2, De Boisboissel takes us to the military world where more and more robots and artificial intelligence are being introduced in war equipment and vehicles and operations are increasingly commanded remotely from the battlefield. The author explores the questions raised by this evolution, especially regarding responsibilities, decision-making and ethics. Based on these insights from the military, Laroche and Reuzeau derive, in Chap. 3, six main takeaway points that civilian organisations could reflect upon.

In Chap. 4, Allspaw takes us behind the scenes of digital devices, more specifically of critical digital services, Internet-connected services that have taken on greater importance in the functioning of society. The author proposes an original perspective on this recent domain by looking at it as a safety–critical field and presents the challenges but also opportunities and advantages that it offers.

Stian Antonsen, in Chap. 5, somehow moderates the enthusiasm towards digitalisation. The author comes back to the scope, capabilities and biases of artificial intelligence, especially compared to human intelligence, and puts them into perspective with the expectations in terms of safety from high-risk industries. He highlights a number of paradoxes that will need to be addressed before AI is used in safety–critical decision-making.

Moving to the impacts of socioeconomic evolution on safety, a number of chapters reflect upon the challenges posed, especially to safety, by the demographic evolution in terms of career length and competence aspects.

Chapter 6, authored by Tosé and Tazi, presents the current situation in Japan where the retirement age was recently pushed back to 70 and will be pushed even further, to 75, in the near future. What Japan is facing today could give a flavour of what other countries could experience in the coming decade and thereby could serve as a source of inspiration. The authors address some of the challenges such as skills and knowledge updating, keeping an interest in work for all generations or managing the mix of generations, which could in turn impact safety. As they envisage to turn senior people into trainers, in Chap. 7, Navarro Rodriguez and Largier highlight the conditions needed to support this mentoring activity for seniors, based on research work done in France and more specifically in the nuclear industry.

The two following Chaps. 8 and 9 put a special emphasis on competencies. In Chap. 8, Pons, Rodriguez and Reuzeau share the work launched by Airbus in 2018 to "meet the future competence challenge" as emphasised by the chapter's title. In Chap. 9, Largier comes back to what competences entail. He underlines the importance of reaching beyond a purely managerial approach and considers organisational dimensions to account for how competencies are actually mobilised and developed individually but also collectively in work situations.

Barcellini, in Chap. 10, reflects upon the management of work transformation when introducing new technologies to avoid repeating pitfalls experienced in the past. She suggests considering the design of future work as a transition process that involves several dimensions—social, organisational, technological—that all need to be addressed to shape a "future of work".

The societal and sociopolitical evolution is touched upon by Baram and Bieder in Chap. 11, through the prism of regulation of high-risk industries. The authors explain how the self-regulation initiated a few decades ago is in the process of being pushed to the extreme and leading to the subordination of safety regulation to industrial leadership on risk governance issues, setting back the role of society on these matters.

The evolutions addressed in the various chapters and referred to earlier in this chapter are not independent from one another, making the overall context a complex and dynamic landscape in which unique human capabilities may well be essential for keeping high-risk industries safe. This is what Shorrock reminds us in Chap. 12, drawing seven learning points from clinicians testimonies on their experience of working under rapidly changing conditions during the COVID-19 pandemic.

Lastly, Chap. 13 by Pariès attempts to draw some lines of thought and action on the management of future safety challenges from the insights provided by the previous chapters. It especially reflects upon the gap between the levels at which major changes shaping the future of high-risk industries are decided and occur and that at which safety is discussed.

References

1. P.G. Almklov, Situated practice and safety as objects of management, in *Beyond Safety Training*. (Springer, Cham, 2018), pp. 59–72
2. T.C. Callari, C. Bieder, B. Kirwan, What is it like for a middle manager to take safety into account? Practices and challenges. Saf. Sci. **113**, 19–29 (2019)
3. S.W. Dekker, The bureaucratization of safety. Saf. Sci. **70**, 348–357 (2014)
4. P.T. Hudson, Safety management and safety culture: the long, hard and winding road, in *Occupational Health and Safety Management Systems* (Crowne Content, Melbourne, 2001)
5. P. Lindøe, M. Baram, G.S. Braut, Risk regulation and proceduralization: an assessment of Norwegian and US risk regulation in offshore oil and gas industry, in *Trapping Safety into Rules* (CRC Press, 2013), pp. 69–86
6. N. Matyjasik, M. Guenoun, *En finir avec le New Public Management* (Institut de la gestion publique et du développement économique, 2019)
7. J. Rasmussen, Risk management in a dynamic society: a modelling problem. Saf. Sci. **27**(2), 183–213 (1997)
8. P. Schulman, E. Roe, M.V. Eeten, M.D. Bruijne, High reliability and the management of critical infrastructures. J. Contingencies Crisis Manag. **12**(1), 14–28 (2004)
9. L. Willcocks, Robo-Apocalypse cancelled? Reframing the automation and future of work debate. J. Inf. Technol. **35**(4), 286–302 (2020)

Open Access This chapter is licensed under the terms of the Creative Commons Attribution 4.0 International License (http://creativecommons.org/licenses/by/4.0/), which permits use, sharing, adaptation, distribution and reproduction in any medium or format, as long as you give appropriate credit to the original author(s) and the source, provide a link to the Creative Commons license and indicate if changes were made.

The images or other third party material in this chapter are included in the chapter's Creative Commons license, unless indicated otherwise in a credit line to the material. If material is not included in the chapter's Creative Commons license and your intended use is not permitted by statutory regulation or exceeds the permitted use, you will need to obtain permission directly from the copyright holder.

Chapter 2
Evolution in the Way of Waging War for Combatants and Military Leaders

Gérard de Boisboissel

Abstract The revolution in systems autonomy is underway. We are at the dawn of a radical change in the use we make of the equipment available to us, with the upcoming and progressive autonomy of this equipment allowing it to adapt to the situation. The danger and complexity of the military world makes it difficult to anticipate the major issues linked to the adoption of these machines, in particular that of the responsibility of the leaders who will allocate their tasks or missions, as well as that of those who design and test these systems. This chapter proposes to list some of the safeguards necessary for their use: the control of these systems by leaders, the necessary confidence in their use and the need to integrate into their embedded software rules to be respected when tasks are executed (rules of engagement linked to the circumstances, or standards not to be violated). It emphasises the absolute role of leaders whose choices must, at all times, prevail over those of AIs, especially in complex situations, and who must ensure the conduct of the manoeuver because they are the guarantor who gives meaning to military action.

Keywords Military · Autonomy · AI · Responsibility · Confidence · Control · Rules · Safeguards

2.1 Introduction

We are on the cusp of a major but inevitable evolution in the delegation of tasks to machines, which is already underway in the civilian word. Technological evolutions represented by robots, artificial intelligence, remote storage and remote processing of information also have strong impacts on military organisations. Battlefield equipment and vehicles will be increasingly digitised and military actions more and more displaced. New tools imply new usages, and new usages imply new doctrines [6]. The way war is conducted is thus undergoing major changes.

G. de Boisboissel (✉)
Saint-Cyr Military Academy Research Centre, Guer, France
e-mail: gerard.de-boisboissel@st-cyr.terre-net.defense.gouv.fr

2.2 Foreseen Changes in the Way of Conducting War

With the volume of information constantly increasing, the need for data processing capable of collecting, receiving and disseminating this information is a key evolution for the armies.

The number of combat functions remotely performed by robots will gradually increase, eventually including the use of lethal effector offsets. As an example, France can no longer do without drones in military operations, especially in Mali where it must cover a very large territory with 5000 soldiers. Recently, jihadist leaders were killed thanks to the contribution of armed drones.

2.2.1 Displacement of the Combatant's Action

Military robots, new tactical tools made available to the armed forces and the combatant, offer several advantages: permanent reporting by sensors, remote effectors, omnipresence of the machine on the battlefield; delegating repetitive or specific tasks usually performed by humans on the battlefield to the machine; as well as a lower exposure to danger for the soldier which meets the demands of nations to preserve and protect their military personnel.

Furthermore, as with the development of artificial intelligence, machines will progressively acquire capacities to analyse the situation, ultimately allowing them to handle the unexpected and adapt to the environment and to the unknown, which is a move towards autonomy, although it must remain under supervision. Once the success rate of the algorithm becomes indisputably better than that of the best human operators, it will be difficult to refute the fact that algorithms are more efficient than humans.

The autonomy of the systems will also be favoured by the fact that robotic autonomous systems are faster and more reactive than humans, especially in case of emergencies requiring very fast reaction times; able to defend themself in response to an aggression; more precise than humans and capable of operating around the clock, subject to energy autonomy.

A new concept of Hyperwar was presented by General John R. Allen, former commander of the NATO International Security Assistance Force and U.S. Forces—Afghanistan (USFOR-A), in 2019. It is based on the time reduction of the decision process [1].

Migration from remote control of machines to automation is inevitable for these reasons, as well as to reduce operator cognitive load and free their movement.

2.2.2 A New Threat: Access to Innovation by Enemies

One major expected change is that robots on the battlefield will level the asymmetry and equalise the balance of power between states or governmental organisations.

To give some examples, a drone (Unmanned Aerial Vehicle) can scout and spot any weaknesses in the protection of a site from the air, using image identification algorithms that make it possible to find targets such as vehicles or people. Swarms of drones can enter a building without the assistance of a global navigation satellite system (GNSS). Drones also can be used as weapons with an explosive charge that can be remotely activated.

The fact is that today the technology to piece together and assemble components to produce such robots is freely available on the Internet. Information is available about the technology for manually piloted robots to fully autonomous robots, from unarmed to armed systems. Most of these new technologies are available in open source, which raises the question of their dissemination and use by many countries and by terrorist groups.

2.2.3 How to Avoid Dissemination?

Faced with such threats, ways must be found to prevent dissemination. One option is to make it compulsory to include the presence of a "secure element" inside the hardware of robots, using it to sign any embedded software, then require robot manufacturers to accept software updates only from a verified server, as is done for smartphone applications like the Google Play "app store" for example.

Drones coming from suppliers and countries not accepting these regulations could be prohibited from sale in democratic countries.

2.3 Impact on Responsibilities

New tools imply new uses, new uses imply new doctrines, and robots are no exception to this rule. One of the challenges will therefore consist in defining a doctrine for use of these robotic systems, starting from existing military doctrines and adapting them to the characteristics of the combat of the future.

2.3.1 Changes at the Organisational Level

Considering any robot as a partner implies changes at the organisational level, namely a reorganisation of military units to better adapt them to the use of these robots. This could include hiring some extra human resources to pilot or supervise robots and the corresponding training. Or transforming existing ways of conducting a military operation, such as, for example, military convoys that could be gradually automated.

2.3.2 Still the Need for Human Responsibility When Using the Machine

Leaders are the human keys of any military action. They give meaning to it, remain responsible for the manoeuvring and the conduct of the war, and adapt "en conduite" depending on events. For that, they must "feel" the battlefield, doing everything to reduce being overwhelmed by the fog of war and the uncertainty and threats.

With the use of robotic weapons systems with an autonomous decision-making capacity, they are then able to delegate tasks or missions to these systems, according to the tactical situation.

Because of that, leaders should remain masters of the action because, unlike machines, they can give meaning to the action and take responsibility for it.

2.3.3 Responsibility is also Common to All Stakeholders

Laws are made in such a way that for any use of autonomous machinery, we need to be able to clearly identify a responsible natural or legal person. In 2012, Keith Miller initiated and led a collective effort to develop a set of rules for "moral responsibility for computer artefacts" [3].

In our study, we will list three levels of responsibility.

2.3.3.1 Responsibility During the Design Phase

- Designers and developers should apply a precautionary principle when developing the algorithms of autonomous systems;
- designers should build humanisation into the designed system when they elaborate its doctrine of use, which means enabling the possibility for the operator to be in the loop;
- they should limit the use of the machine to what it is made for, and the environment in which it is made to operate;
- any autonomy for a system must be limited to a defined space and time for its use;
- designers must ensure it is possible to remotely neutralise a machine in the event of loss of control, or internally if its embedded software "recognises" that a situation is unexpected and potentially dangerous.

2.3.3.2 Responsibility of the Leaders, the People Using Their Judgement to Determine the Best Option for Using It and When

- The human and the machine have to train altogether to form a single military entity;
- the leaders should prepare the mission in advance with a tactical reasoning that includes these machines from the start of the mission until its end;
- the leaders will precisely define the rules of engagement of the machine, namely the conditions of activation and the constraints to be respected by these systems, while limiting their activation in time and space.

2.3.3.3 Responsibility of the Operators

- Operators must ask themselves whether the use of the system is appropriate before its activation on the battlefield, and, if it is weaponised, about the proportionality of an armed response;
- the operators have the closest situational awareness, and, although the machine can make probability calculations, probability does not take into account the complexity of military situations on the battlefield, which require human analysis.

2.4 The Place of Leaders in Complex Systems

The delegation of tasks to increasingly autonomous machines raises the question of the place of the humans who interface these systems and should remain in control of them.

2.4.1 Leaders Must Always Control the Use of an Autonomous System

It is a fact that the military will not use equipment or tools that they do not control, and this applies to all armies around the world. Military leaders must be in control of the military action, and to this end, must be able to control the units and the means at their disposal. Military leaders place their confidence in them to carry out the mission, which is the basis of the principle of subsidiarity.

For this reason, it is not in their interest to have a robotic system that governs itself with its own rules and objectives, nor one that is disobedient or can break out of the framework that has been set for it. Similarly, such a system must respect military orders and instructions. The consequence is that at any time leaders must be able to regain control of a robotic system and potentially cause it to leave the "autonomous mode" in which they themselves had authorised it to enter.

Therefore, machines with a certain degree of autonomy must be subordinate to the chain of command and subject to orders, counter orders and reporting.

2.4.2 Operators Must Have Confidence When Delegating Tasks to an Autonomous System

The military will never use equipment or tools that they do not trust. This is why leaders must have confidence in the way a machine behaves or could behave. Consequently, military engineers should develop autonomous systems capable of explaining their decisions.

Automatic systems are predictable, and we can easily anticipate how they will perform the task entrusted to them. However, it becomes more complex with autonomous systems, especially self-learning systems where the objective of the task to be accomplished by the machine is known but not how it will operate. This poses a serious question of confidence in this system. When I ask an autonomous robot lawn mower to mow my lawn, I know my lawn will be mown, but I don't know how the robot will proceed exactly.

The best examples to focus on are the soldier's expectations about artificial intelligence (AI) embedded in autonomous systems.

- AI should be trustable. This means that adaptive and self-learning systems must be able to explain their reasoning and decisions to human operators in a transparent and understandable manner;
- AI should be explainable and predictable: you must understand the different steps of reasoning carried out by a machine that solves a problem for you or provides an answer to a complex question. For that, we need a human–machine interface (HMI) explaining its decision-making mechanism.

We therefore have to focus on more transparent and personalised human–machine interfaces at the service of users and leaders.

2.4.3 Cognitive Overload: The Need for a Digital Assistant

The digitisation of the battlefield began several years ago with weapon systems, vehicles and military equipment. One of its consequences is that it may generate information overload for leaders who are already very busy and focused on their tasks of commanding and managing. There is consensus within the military community that leaders can manage a maximum of seven different information sources at the same time, and fewer when under fire.

Delegating is one way to avoid cognitive overload, and one possible solution is to create a "digital assistant" who can assist leaders in the stages of information processing.

This assistant can initially be a person, a deputy who will manage the data generated by the battlefield. Then in some decades, the assistant may become digital, i.e. an autonomous machine that will assist leaders in filtering and processing information, and be a decision-making aid for them.

2.4.4 AI Will Influence the Decisions Made by the Leader

Stress is an inherent component of taking responsibility. It is common for military leaders to feel overwhelmed in a complex military situation. In such contexts, leaders will most often be inclined to trust a source of artificial intelligence because they will consider it, provided they have confidence in it, to be a serious decision-making aid that is not influenced by any stress, with superior processing capabilities and the ability to test multiple combinations for a particular effect.

The fact remains that any self-learning system must be taught. Military leaders will also be responsible for the proper learning and use of self-learning machinery in the field. To do so, they will have to supervise the learning process prior to its regular use and ensure its control over time.

2.5 New Rules for Autonomous Systems

Considering the major potential effects of systems with a certain form of autonomy on the battlefield, they should be constrained by new rules.

2.5.1 Machines Have to Respect Law Rules

Any military action must respect the different rules and constraints linked to the environment in which it takes place. Which means necessary supervision on the deontological, ethical and legal aspects.

For the military, these rules and constraints are manifold [2]:

- the legal constraint linked to international regulations, in particular respect for the rules of international humanitarian law (principle of humanity, discrimination, precaution, proportionality and necessity). All military leaders are responsible for the means they engage on the battlefield and their use. Binding Article 36 of the additional protocol to the Geneva Convention stipulates that any new weapon system must be lawful;

- the rules of engagement (ROE) formulated by military leaders depending on the context.[1] In particular for any critical action such as opening fire, and other such decisions which involve personal responsibility;
- professional ethical constraints, namely an ethical imperative that military leaders apply according to the situation on the battlefield. These constraints emanate from the authority employing the autonomous systems.

2.5.2 Hardware and Components Should Be Protected by Design

To ensure that the above rules are respected, it is essential to limit the framework of execution of the embedded software of autonomous systems. One possible solution is to integrate constraints "by design" in the initial design of the machine, such as execution safeguards in the hardware or the software, anticipating the worst-case scenario and ensuring they cannot occur.

2.5.2.1 Conception: Safeguards Within the Software Development Process

The following recommendations for designing systems having some form of autonomy have been inspired from document [6]:

- follow design methodologies that clearly define responsibilities;
- ensure the control of the various possible reactions of the machine. To do that, when a formal approach is too difficult, limit it to a corpus of known situations where a decision can be modelled[2];
- frame the execution of the algorithms by defining red lines that must not be crossed relating to:
  - technological constraints;
  - rules to follow such as ethics or legal rules;
  - unwanted or unpredictable behaviours.
- restrict the autonomy of these systems by implementing embedded software safeguards, designed to ensure that these red lines are never crossed.

---

[1] ROE are military directives that delineate when, where, how and against whom military force may be used, and they have implications for what actions soldiers may take on their own authority and what directives may be issued by a commanding officer.

[2] Formal methods are mathematically rigorous techniques that contribute to the reliability and robustness of a design.

2.5.2.2 Certification

In the case of autonomous systems, the complexity of their algorithms complicates the traditional approach to simulation testing. It is necessary to verify whether the autonomy of the robot can be diverted from its original purpose, voluntarily or involuntarily.

Moreover, it is rarely possible to carry out tests by controlling the entire information-processing chain within the device. Many evaluations are conducted in "black boxes", which means that the evaluator can only control the test environment, i.e. the stimuli to be sent to the system, and observe the output behaviours.

As there is a general wish for transparency and control over the behaviour certification of the systems, there is a clearly identified need to set a formal and rigorous framework for the evaluation of these devices, and it is thus preferable to develop white box algorithms to facilitate their certification.

2.5.2.3 Ethics

The consideration of ethical issues in the development, maintenance and execution of software becomes an imperative in the context of the autonomy of robotics systems.

A machine is by nature amoral. The human being remains the one and only moral agent, therefore the only responsible.

In which case, should we be able to code ethical rules? This seems impossible, because ethical reasoning requires situational awareness and consciousness, which are uniquely human characteristics [5]. Nevertheless, the integration of partial ethical reasoning into a machine can be considered. This would amount to designing an artificial agent belonging to a human–robot system capable of having computer reasoning that takes into account the law rules to be respected (see above) and able to make a decision as well as explain it to an operator. Catherine Tessier describes in [6] three different approaches:

- a consequentialist framework which focuses on the effect and therefore the finality;
- an ethical framework that focuses on the means for obtaining the effects;
- a deontological approach (knowing that military deontology is to respect the adversary and minimise casualties).

Notwithstanding the extreme difficulty in developing these approaches, this raises the question of how to organise the hierarchy of values.

2.6 Towards an International Standardisation

In a scenario where human beings move away from the decision-making process, in favour of machines, it is necessary to decide how to define a common base of ethical rules applicable at the international level, which in turn consists of two levels: the civilian and the military.

2.6.1 Civilian Level

At the civilian level, the Institute of Electrical and Electronics Engineers (IEEE) Ethically Aligned Design Document elevates the importance of ethics in the development of artificial intelligence (AI) and autonomous systems (AS) [4].

The possibility of digitally encoding ethics and making the algorithm of an autonomous system react in accordance with ethics from the human point of view is a very difficult subject of research. Indeed, it requires ethicists to translate ethical reasoning into algorithmic thought. This would seem very difficult still, except as explained above, by framing and safeguarding the possibilities of autonomous actions of the machine.

Moreover, different peoples have different ethics. Who has the legitimacy to determine the best criteria of ethical behaviour? And can we consider as acceptable a personalised ethics knowing that abuses are always possible?

2.6.2 Military Level

At the military level, ethical approaches are different as the objective of the armed forces is to be efficient on the battlefield, perform the missions entrusted to them, while respecting rules.

Looking at the international level, we are now witnessing a race for autonomous technologies. States will want to make sure that they take advantage of these systems, but regarding ethics, answers will vary. Liberal states will have to deal with the temptation of efficiency versus ethical constraints, while some totalitarian states will have a different response to these challenges, particularly for countries with a collective and not an individual ethic.

2.6.3 Lethal Autonomous Weapon Systems

While armed drones can limit collateral damage thanks to their precision, the question of delegating the opening of fire to lethal autonomous weapon systems (LAWS) is a question that has particular resonance in the international debate and raises the question of moral acceptance of autonomous weapons.

The author of this chapter thinks that LAWS are justifiable in the case of saturated threats, air or (sub)marine combat, in areas of total prohibition of human presence while limited in time and space. The author believes there is a need for operators to control LAWS, thus rendering such systems semi-autonomous (LSAWS). The ethical question of their use shifts to the level of the military decision-maker who will decide on the delegation of the activation of the "semi-autonomous fire" mode to the system [6].

2.7 Conclusion

Today, we are witnessing the first elements of a real revolution in the art of war. New robotic military equipment will progressively become autonomous and adapt to the terrain to accomplish their assigned missions.

This implies changes at the doctrinal and organisational levels and will challenge the role of leaders on the battlefield. Their credibility will depend on their ability to exercise authority over the human resources entrusted to them and on the control of the autonomous robots placed at their disposal, their conscience allowing them to humanise war, where the machine has no soul.

The development of new autonomous systems raises the question of controlling their proliferation for military uses, which may take the form of a binding international legal framework to restrict potential uses that do not comply with international rules.

But technological competition is repeating itself, and it is ineluctable that several states will try to impose their technological sovereignty through the development of these autonomous robots.

References

1. G.J. Allen, *Hyperwar Is Coming* (USFOR-A, 2019). Retrieved from https://www.youtube.com/watch?v=ofYWf2SKd_c
2. D. Danet, G. de Boisboissel, R. Doaré, *Drones et Killer robots: faut-il les interdire?* (Presses Universitaires de Rennes, 2015)
3. F. Grodzinsky, K. Miller, M. Wolf, Moral responsibility for computing artifacts: "the rules" and issues of trust. ACM SIGCAS Comput. Soc. **42**(2), 15–25 (2012). https://doi.org/10.1145/2422509.2422511
4. IEEE, *Ethically Aligned Design*, 2nd edn. (Institute of Electrical and Electronics Engineers, 2017). Retrieved from https://standards.ieee.org/content/dam/ieee-standards/standards/web/documents/other/ead_v2.pdf
5. D. Lambert, *Que penser de…? La robotique et l'Intelligence artificielle* (Fidélité, 2020)
6. RDN, Autonomie et létalité en robotique militaire. (CREC, Ed.) *Cahiers de la Revue Défense Nationale* (2018). Retrieved from https://www.defnat.com/e-RDN/sommaire_cahier.php?cid cahier=1166

Open Access This chapter is licensed under the terms of the Creative Commons Attribution 4.0 International License (http://creativecommons.org/licenses/by/4.0/), which permits use, sharing, adaptation, distribution and reproduction in any medium or format, as long as you give appropriate credit to the original author(s) and the source, provide a link to the Creative Commons license and indicate if changes were made.

The images or other third party material in this chapter are included in the chapter's Creative Commons license, unless indicated otherwise in a credit line to the material. If material is not included in the chapter's Creative Commons license and your intended use is not permitted by statutory regulation or exceeds the permitted use, you will need to obtain permission directly from the copyright holder.

Chapter 3
Learning from the Military

Autonomous Systems and Safety in Work and Organisations

Hervé Laroche and Florence Reuzeau

Abstract Moving from the military to civilian organisations, this chapter discusses the key points of Gérard de Boisboissel's contribution about the impact of autonomous systems on safety issues. We comment on these points from two angles: (1) human–system interaction and (2) organisational reliability. Stressing differences in context and in resulting implications, we strongly recommend that the upcoming invasion of work organisations by autonomous systems should be viewed (also) through the lens of the social sciences.

Keywords Human–system interaction · Empowerment · Cognitive overload · Trust · Learning

3.1 Introduction

The purpose of the previous chapter and the present one is to take inspiration from the military about the impact of autonomous systems (high level of automation, AI[1]) on safety issues in civilian organisations. The military has long been a source of inspiration for civilian organisations, providing many reflections and advances in terms of safety. Regarding the impact of autonomous systems on safety, the military can be taken as an extreme case in many respects, given (a) the huge risks involved in military operations, (b) the complex, advanced sociotechnical systems that modern armies have become and (c) the speed and extent to which they are currently investing in the development and implementation of autonomous systems.

Of course, we are not advocating that civil organisations imitate the military in these matters. Taking the military evolutions analysed in the previous chapter as a

---
[1] Artificial intelligence.

H. Laroche (✉)
ESCP Business School, Paris, France
e-mail: laroche@escp.eu

F. Reuzeau
Airbus, Toulouse, France

starting point, our purpose is to discuss the extent to which similar evolutions will apply to industrial organisations and to what extent they will have implications for safety.

3.2 Six Key Points

We extracted six key points from Gérard de Boisboissel's contribution in Chap. 2 (five from the chapter and one from later discussions with the author). For each of these points, we add comments from two angles: (1) human–system interaction (a micro-perspective) and (2) organisational reliability (meso-perspective).

3.2.1 Inevitability

Migration from remote control of machines to highly autonomous systems is inevitable.

Though the magnitude, pervasiveness and speed of such a migration may greatly vary from one industry to another, we agree with this observation. This is why civilian, at-risk organisations should address the following points.

3.2.2 Responsibility and Control

Humans should remain masters of the action because, unlike the machine, they can give meaning to the action and take responsibility for it. The military leader must be able to regain control of a robotic system at any time and potentially cause it to leave the "autonomous mode" in which humans themselves had authorised it to enter.

This is the eternal question about the allocation of tasks between humans and machines. Humans can stay in control of a situation, even though they delegate information-processing or execution tasks to an autonomous machine, under specific conditions, such as being fully engaged in the monitoring of the level of execution of the task. However, if the manager or the operator temporarily delegates the complete task including the decision-making, it will be difficult to immediately regain full control of the situation in case of an event. Even if the machine can deliver detailed information, the manager or operator will face an abundance of "cold" data to be integrated. Regaining mental and emotional control of the situation will be very demanding in terms of cognitive and sensory resources.

Another question is: will the humans always be willing to retake control and thus engage their own responsibility? The answer might not be straightforward, especially in civilian work contexts. Some autonomous systems leave no choice to humans (e.g.

the autopilot disengaging because of incoherent data inputs). Such systems are able to diagnose their own disfunctioning. When this capacity is lacking or is severely restrained, the initiative belongs to the human. Regaining control will thus be a decision made by the human agent. We should not assume that all humans will make the decision to regain full control, at once, in all cases. The decision-makers may have (good or bad) reasons for not doing so. Among them is the anticipation of blame or, more generally, the expected attribution of responsibility between the system and the human. Recent research on this matter has established that failing humans and machines are not judged in the same way [7]. Machines are judged according to the magnitude of the harm, while humans are judged regarding their intentions. This important finding does not indicate a clear answer to our question, but it certainly suggests that, beyond the general human-responsibility principle, regaining control might imply complex human decision-making processes.

3.2.3 Trustability

Autonomous systems should be trustable, explainable and predictable. For humans to trust autonomous systems, adaptive and self-learning systems must be able to explain their reasoning and decisions to human operators in a transparent and understandable manner and must behave consistently over time and circumstances.

Explaining may look like a straightforward notion, but it is quite the reverse. An explanation is not a property of texts, narratives, figures or diagrams. Rather, it stems from a relationship between (1) the text, narrative, figure or diagram that is presented to the recipient, (2) the recipient's cognitive processes, (3) the context and its immediate demands, and (4) the recipient's goals in this context [8, p. 86]. This implies that explainability has to be designed. Such a design has to incorporate user diversity and situation variability. For example, accuracy and thoroughness are not necessarily needed to provide good explanations, that is, explanations that the persons involved will find good. In fact, in many cases providing biased or incomplete explanations might be more relevant in order to make the system explainable [8, p. 89]. Given the resulting challenge, and given that today's knowledge about explainability and its design is very limited, explainability failures will likely occur, with significant consequences on human trust in systems. More generally, we can expect more failures involving some form of knowledge issue (epistemic accidents, as coined by Downer [4]—see also Antonsen, this volume).

Beyond explanation information, the requirements for synchronising humans and autonomous systems need to be developed to foster an efficient human–machine teaming. Inspired by the human–human cooperation principles [2], human and machine should "share a common context and background" in order to elaborate a common strategic action plan and adjust or redirect its execution in a coordinated way.

To overcome the potential ambiguity of a one-way communication line from human to machine and enable the machine to support the human efficiently, a human–machine dialogue about information, rules or ethics, could be necessary [5]. The machine has to match human intentions to reduce the risk of violating ethics rules or embarking in wrong directions because of design errors.

3.2.4 Self-Learning Machines and Human Training

As military leaders will be responsible for the proper use of a self-learning machine in the field, they must supervise the learning process prior to its regular use and ensure its control over time. To be resilient, the leaders and the operators need to be trained with the technical equipment AND without it (or in degraded mode). This is very costly.

On the one hand, a self-learning machine principle on the field can be a way to capture the variability of operations, the diversity of situations and operators' experiences. On the other hand, being trained by a human can be risky if human perception and representation biases are integrated into the machine.

More generally, it should be recalled that, though widely advocated, the need for extensive human training, unfortunately, is still largely ignored by industrial organisations. Autonomous systems only reinforce the need to question usual forms of safety training and go far beyond mandatory training [3].

3.2.5 Cognitive Overload

Delegating is one way of avoiding the military leader's cognitive overload. One possible solution is to create a "digital assistant" who can assist the leader in the information-processing steps.

Machines are becoming more and more sophisticated. Either human–machine interaction requires specific skills or the interaction is complex and can divert operators' attention away from their main task, reducing the added value of the human operator. Cognitive overload is much less common in civilian organisations than in combat. Yet the idea of a specialised technician assisting the decision-maker still makes sense and in fact is rather common: think of the radiologist and the technician operating the scanner, for instance. Yet, in real life, what will happen between the decision-maker and the assistant? Barley's classic work reminds us that (1) the actual division of labour may depart significantly from the designed work organisation; (2) the actual division of labour results from complex social processes that lead to different outcomes in different contexts; these outcomes are largely unpredictable [1]. Alleviating the cognitive load is traded for sociopolitical processes. Better mastery of action is not a guaranteed outcome.

3.2.6 Empowerment Paradox

Autonomous systems generally imply an empowerment for operators relative to leaders, because operators benefit from increased capacities and/or may dedicate themselves to higher level tasks. However, autonomous systems can also be designed so that leaders are able to recover full control at any moment—taking it from the hands of the operator. Empowered operators thus can be made powerless at any moment.

Autonomous systems displace the division of control and transform its dynamics. When and why could leaders be tempted to take direct control? With what consequences? The empowerment paradox reminds us that, if human trust in a system is certainly an issue, human trust in fellow humans will remain a major issue too. What would have happened at Fukushima Daichi if Tepco managers and Prime Minister Kan had had the possibility to take direct and full control of the onsite operations and move aside Yoshida, the local director? They probably would have taken control and made major mistakes. Managers, just like military leaders, are prone to illusions of control (i.e. the tendency to overestimate one's degree of control over a course of action). Autonomous systems reinforce this bias, if only because, by design, increased control is one of their strongest promises—as advertised by those who manufacture and sell these systems to top executives. The issue is not intractable, though. Some professional experts are granted a degree of autonomy that can never be overridden by any hierarchy. Similar designs can be implemented for operators or lower-level managers working with an autonomous system. Even if top managers are still technically able to take full control, they would then commit a violation and expose themselves to dire consequences in case of failure.

The articulation of autonomous systems and human beings should be considered in the context of hierarchy and power in organisations. Autonomous systems could very well revive the old dream that was fueled by the development of the first computers. Humans would be in control at the very top of the organisation (overall objectives and strategy) and at the very bottom (execution of tasks). All the intermediate levels would be under the power of automatic systems. To a certain extent, this was already Taylor's ambition, with a workforce of engineers equipped with methods for designing work processes instead of computers or autonomous systems. The sociology of organisations has taught us that employees will fight to avoid being replaced by autonomous systems or the loss of status and independence that autonomous systems might imply. Many will probably lose this fight. However, skilled workers and experts working through or with autonomous systems will detain the practical knowledge that is required to make these systems efficient and safe. They will use this knowledge to their own advantage in the power struggles with their bosses and other constituencies. Just like front-line operators quickly learn to game the rules and procedures that they are supposed to follow, knowledge workers will likely engage in various, covert manoeuvers to game the autonomous systems and retain control over key stakes for their occupational groups [6]. Wherever autonomous systems are expected to improve safety in comparison with humans, this political struggle is likely to bend the expected functioning just like it does today. Humans will game autonomous systems just like they game the rules of bureaucracy, with the resulting effects of creating safety issues. Conversely, in the same way that gaming procedures or systems can be good for safety in some situations, gaming autonomous systems will sometimes prove good for safety. The overall outcome is unpredictable.

3.3 Final Comments

Organisations are already, in some way, autonomous systems. Military leaders, managers and operators are already working with (or within) automated, autonomous systems. The machine stops, the operator calls maintenance, maintenance is provided, and the machine works again. Maintenance is an autonomous system for the operator, even though they do not think of maintenance in these terms, but rather as the individuals providing the service. There is no difference of nature between working with an autonomous system and relying on an operational unit, a functional department, a piece of software or a combination of all these—which is what everybody does every day in today's organisations. The digital autonomous systems that will be implemented in the next 10 or 20 years will not change the nature of actions produced in and by organisations. Consequently, we will encounter the same types of safety issues that we have encountered to date. So nothing will change. And yet, of course, everything will change because these systems will profoundly affect the division of work, the distribution of knowledge, the coordination processes, the political balances and many other key variables in the functioning of organisations and in the achievement of safety. Same game, same rules, different players and maybe—that is the question—different outcomes. As K. E. Weick wrote: "Planes don't fly. Organisations fly airplanes". Similarly, organisations run autonomous systems that run autonomous systems. Maybe one day autonomous systems will run organisations, but this is not likely in the near future.

One key implication of this view is that the upcoming invasion of work organisations by autonomous systems should be viewed (also) through the lens of the social sciences. In fact, it seems that, in comparison with the past, the industrial world is increasingly calling on the social sciences to question the digital transformation and identify the issues for the human operator and organisations. It should be helpful to carefully consider if and how evolutions can be easily accepted (or not) and embodied by operators.

References

1. S.R. Barley, Technology as an occasion for structuring: evidence from observations of CT scanners and the social order of radiology departments. Adm. Sci. Q. 78–108 (1986)
2. D. Bernard, Cognitive interaction with virtual assistants: from philosophical foundations to illustrative examples in aeronautics. Comput. Ind. **107**, 33–49 (2019)
3. C. Bieder, C. Gilbert, B. Journé, H. Laroche, *Beyond Safety Training: Embedding Safety in Professional Skills* (Springer, 2017)
4. J. Downer, "737-Cabriolet": the limits of knowledge and the sociology of inevitable failure. Am. J. Sociol. **117**(3), 725–762 (2011)
5. European Commission, *Ethics Guidelines for Trustworthy AI* (2019). Retrieved from https://digital-strategy.ec.europa.eu/library/ethics-guidelines-trustworthy-ai
6. S. Faraj, S. Pachidi, K. Sayegh, Working and organizing in the age of the learning algorithm. Inf. Organ. **28**(1), 62–70 (2018)
7. C.A. Hidalgo, D. Orghiain, J.A. Canals, F. De Almeida, N. Martín, *How Humans Judge Machines* (MIT Press, 2021)
8. S.T. Mueller, R.R. Hoffman, W. Clancey, A. Emrey, G. Klein, *Explanation in Human-AI Systems: A Literature Meta-Review, Synopsis of Key Ideas and Publications, and Bibliography for Explainable AI* (C. University, Editor) (2019). Retrieved from arXiv.org: https://arxiv.org/abs/1902.01876

Open Access This chapter is licensed under the terms of the Creative Commons Attribution 4.0 International License (http://creativecommons.org/licenses/by/4.0/), which permits use, sharing, adaptation, distribution and reproduction in any medium or format, as long as you give appropriate credit to the original author(s) and the source, provide a link to the Creative Commons license and indicate if changes were made.

The images or other third party material in this chapter are included in the chapter's Creative Commons license, unless indicated otherwise in a credit line to the material. If material is not included in the chapter's Creative Commons license and your intended use is not permitted by statutory regulation or exceeds the permitted use, you will need to obtain permission directly from the copyright holder.

Chapter 4
Critical Digital Services

An Under-Studied Safety-Critical Domain

John Allspaw

Abstract While the COVID-19 pandemic has brought new attention to how essential Internet-connected services are to society's functioning, there continues to be a dearth of research about how these critical digital services (CDSs) are operated, maintained, and delivered from a cognitive work, human factors, and safety science perspective. Efforts to anticipate what the future of work will look like must consider the challenges and opportunities this now critical domain faces. The conditions are favorable for making progress in studying work in this domain. A small (but growing) community of practitioners in software engineering and operations are enthusiastic about exploring and understanding the *cognitive work* they engage in every day. There is also (at least, currently) a relative *absence* of regulatory or procedural barriers that would otherwise hamper productive exploration by researchers.

Keywords Critical digital services · Software engineering · Online operations · Automation

4.1 Introduction

It might appear self-evident, perhaps even banal, to say that *all* modern businesses rely on Internet-connected services. The societal need to adapt to the global COVID-19 pandemic has highlighted how much organizations have come to rely on distributed software applications in many facets of everyday life. For example, to follow social distancing policies (which prevented working in offices), many adapted by working from their homes using video conferencing and other collaboration tools (such as messaging and chat services). Many smartphone and tablet users who have viewed these applications as *conveniences* suddenly realized how integral they have become for keeping some of the most fundamental societal functioning alive in many countries worldwide. Services such as:

J. Allspaw (✉)
Adaptive Capacity Labs, New York, USA
e-mail: allspaw@adaptivecapacitylabs.com

© The Author(s) 2022
H. Laroche et al. (eds.), *Managing Future Challenges for Safety*,
SpringerBriefs in Safety Management,
https://doi.org/10.1007/978-3-031-07805-7_4

- food and medicine delivery apps;
- social media and community organizing/communication services;
- news and broadcasting channels;
- information, data, and guidance published by governments;
- new channels of coordination between research organizations working on vaccines.

all became critical to supporting both local and global communities.

While the COVID-19 pandemic certainly played a critical role in highlighting how essential these services are, the importance of these digital services has been growing for some time.

Many (if not all) high-tempo and high-consequence industries (energy, transportation, medicine, aviation, etc.) have experienced surprising disruptions significant enough to be later seen as *seminal* accidents (Three-Mile Island, Chernobyl, Tenerife airport disaster, etc.). These events presented such a major shock to the prevailing ideas on what constitutes risk and safety that they upended previous beliefs held by those studying or practicing work in those domains. As David Woods has said, these events revealed that "things didn't work the way we thought they did" (personal communication, July 20, 2021).

The industries associated with these now well-known accidents learned *the hard way* that controlling risk of accidents required understanding the "messy details" of real work done by people in their given roles and the organizational framing (management, leadership, etc.) that influences that work.

Critical digital services has yet to experience its "Three-Mile Island" event. Is such an accident necessary for the domain to take human performance seriously? Or can it translate what other domains have learned and make productive use of those lessons to inform how work is done and risk is anticipated for the future? The answers to these questions are currently unclear, but we can start by exploring what opportunities and challenges CDS has that contrast with other domains.

4.2 Growing Criticality

If we look closely at those domains traditionally known as "safety–critical" mentioned above, we will find a great deal of dependence on software services delivered across the Internet.

For example, if electronic medical health record systems are unavailable or experiencing latency, this disruption can significantly impact hospital operations, which then require staff to implement workarounds. Unfortunately, in many cases, these workarounds must be in place without knowing how long they will be necessary.

In the U.S. alone, e-commerce sales grew 20-fold between 2000 and 2019. The estimated value of the U.S. digital economy was USD 1.35 trillion in 2017. Rates of data transfer (in aggregate) grew from 0.1 terabytes per second (TB/s) in 2002 to 45 TB/s in 2017 and are expected to reach 150 TB/s by 2022.

4.3 Growing Consequences

We need not look further than daily news channels for demonstrations of this criticality. The effects of outages, degradations, and other types of disturbances can range from a short-lived inconvenience to unrecoverable, viability-crushing events for companies. These disruptions can also have devastating *cascading* consequences long after responders have restored service. Consider complications that can exist in the aftermath of:

- **airline reservation systems** (effects on crew scheduling, flight logistics, etc.) [11];
- **stock exchanges** (effects on equity pricing, financial solvency, etc.) [10];
- **electronic medical health records** (effects on clinical procedures, bed capacity, etc.) [15];
- **entertainment and sporting events** (effects on fan behaviors, crowd controls, etc.) [13];
- **retail businesses** (effects on regional economics, employment, etc.) [5].

4.4 The Landscape of Roles and Skills

To make informed projections about the challenges that CDSs are likely to face in the future, it is worthwhile to describe how roles and professions have evolved over time.

In the early days of the web, much of the work involved with designing, building, and operating Internet-connected services was typically done by *generalists*, most coming from a programming background. Once the web (and the technologies that powered it) took on new capabilities and the global userbase grew, specializations began to appear. The generalist role of "webmaster" disappeared and new ones emerged that fell into two categories: *application development* (focused on user-facing) functionality and *systems administration* (focused on underlying operating systems and other infrastructure.)

In the early 2000s, Web sites took on more interactive functionality. Advances in network connectivity, web-specific programming languages, new standards, and other new technologies fueled the development and growth of even more complicated uses. Web *sites* became web *applications* and the use of databases to store and retrieve data exploded. Database administration became a specialized role, and as e-commerce businesses grew in use and scale, so did the need for network and security engineering roles.

Specialist roles and skills continue to emerge, but they continue to sit roughly in two main areas. "Front-end" engineers focus largely on software related to the functionality, design, and representation of user-facing interfaces. "Back-end" engineers focus on the technical infrastructure that supports and enables the front-end applications to work, such as operating systems, languages, databases, and other architectural components that are typically invisible to users of the service.

These specialized skills and roles evolve and adapt very effectively—practitioner communities grow and organize in a bottoms-up and organic fashion (via collaborating on open-source code, conferences, etc.), rather than via centralized professional organizations like those found in aviation or medicine.

While there has been some effort to provide formal training, accreditation, and licensure of these skills [12], they have not been successful. There has been much debate about the need for formalized training and licensure for these roles. The most significant barriers are seen as the relative immaturity of the field (despite its growing criticality) and what assurances licensing could practically give in such a fast-moving field of practice.

A notable aspect in CDS worlds that contrast with others is that quite often, the *designer* of technology is also the *operator* or *user* of the technology. This is in stark contrast to what is found in other domains. Take, for example, medical monitoring devices found in clinical settings. These are not designed (or even modified in ways beyond the built-in controls) by the doctors or nurses who use them every day, but by manufacturers at a distance. In CDS environments, engineers often create new software tools for their own use or modify the existing tools they use. Engineers who find a need for new functionality in the tools they use will simply write that new functionality into the tool, sometimes on the spot.

Why and how does this matter? It means the feedback between user and designer in the same individual is quite fluid (and largely tacit) and interfaces can evolve at a rapid pace as a result. This tool-creating and modifying capacity in the CDS domain is rather unique and represents a great advantage over work done in environments where physical limitations and laws (gravity, thermodynamics, chemical reactions, etc.) govern what can and cannot be modified.

4.5 What Does the Future of Work in CDS Look Like?

Lisanne Bainbridge's seminal paper, *Ironies of Automation* [4], is almost 40 years old and is perhaps more relevant today than it was when it was published. In the 2010s, specialized communities of practice in the tech industry began to emerge, such as "DevOps[1]" and "SRE.[2]" New topics which described the lived experience these practitioners encountered in their work started to appear in conference talks, blog posts, and mailing list discussions. These included subjects such as:

- difficulties with designing and handling alarms or alerts to reduce false positives;
- exploration of novel on-call rotation structures and schedules;

---

[1] Approach aiming at conciliating software development (Dev) and operations (Ops).
[2] Site Reliability Engineer.

- new generations of diagnostic tools to help engineers understand their application and system behaviors;
- approaches to onboard new and early career engineers into such complex environments;
- indicators of occupational burnout and activities that may mitigate it;
- (and many others).

Rather than focus discussions on computer science or programming concerns, it was clear these engineers became enthusiastic and curious about a myriad of topics that professionals from the world of safety would recognize as *human factors* [2].

Fast forwarding to 2021, the SRE and DevOps communities are now established as distinct fields of practice. In the past few years, there has been a faint trickle of research interest on the work these engineers do [1, 7, 9], but there is still much that is unclear.

4.6 What Can Industry Adaptation to COVID-19 Tell Us?

Organizations responsible for producing and operating CDSs needed to adapt quickly in the beginning of 2020 as the pandemic grew worldwide. From a business viability perspective, some online businesses faltered (such as travel-related services) while others saw unprecedented growth (telemedicine, for example).

By and large, the tech industry managed to adapt relatively well to the pandemic relative to other industries. Far and away, the greatest demonstration of this adaptation was adjusting the workforce to work from home and other alternate locations. As mentioned, Internet-capable communication and collaboration tools proved to be integral on this front. Prior to the pandemic, a few notable tech companies differentiated themselves as employers by declaring to be a "remote-friendly" business, with staff distributed across the globe [14]. While many other companies employed a small percentage of staff who worked outside of corporate offices, changing routines and practices that did *not* rely on in-person interactions was difficult.

It became quite clear there was a difference between "working from home" and working from home in a pandemic that required "lockdowns." For those with children who could not attend school or who were primary caregivers for those needing assistance, adjustments were not simply geographical in nature. Managing schedules and calendars became a much more difficult task, in addition to the fatigue generated by prolonged video conferencing.

Despite these multiple challenges, early analysis reveals increases in productivity, especially for those in scientific and technical roles [6].

4.7 A Critical yet Nascent Domain

There are several features of the critical digital services domain worth highlighting, in contrast to others. These qualities represent both challenges and opportunities to researchers.

4.7.1 Challenges

The first challenge is the relative age of the domain. While the invention of technologies and frameworks we now know as the World Wide Web took place in 1989, mainstream adoption began to accelerate several years later. Contrasting this history with transportation industries such as rail and aviation, it is much younger. Many studies taking place currently are novel, rather than building on a corpus of research spanning decades.

Another challenge is the somewhat insular nature of activity among practitioner communities. Despite much research attention brought to more theoretical topics surrounding computer science (such as machine learning and human–computer interaction), the work of software service *operations* tends to be viewed outside and quite different. This may bring groups to be reluctant to participate in research projects.

Modern software—especially applications that are deployed and operated in "open" environments such as the Internet—*cannot* be made to be free of bugs. The variety of usage and complexity of its mechanisms are simply too great to model sufficiently enough to provide assurance that accidents and outages would not happen. To a working engineer in the CDS domain, this fact is assumed in such a fundamental "sky is blue, grass is green" way that it is usually unspoken. Fundamental surprises [8] are common. The challenge for CDS is not that this is the case; it is that outsiders of the community are unaware of how uncertain software's behavior is and how well it can be tested prior to being deployed for use.

Perhaps the most significant challenge is how fast the criticality—and the expertise required to operate the technology to support it—is growing. Researchers looking to characterize and study this work will need to find ways to collect, collate, and synthesize the data they need more efficiently. This world being studied will not wait on twentieth-century research timeframes.

4.7.2 Opportunities and Advantages for Researchers

From a *cognitive work* research perspective, the tech industry's adaptation to work in a more distributed fashion during the pandemic did bring a potential opportunity that was not present prior to the pandemic: an unprecedented abundance of data that might be available for analysis. Since teams working remotely with each other is mediated by software, data that researchers would want or need may be available.

Even the most basic features of current video conferencing, chat, and other collaboration tools include recording and/or logging actions taken, and utterances made by participants, at millisecond granularity. Collecting these *externalizations* for analysis historically was not possible without expensive audio and video recording equipment, and if they were not set up or recording a given exchange, the data were simply missed. The tools used for transcription and analysis have also dramatically improved the data researchers have available to them.

Another significant advantage in this domain is the flip side of the challenge mentioned above: its relative short history. How is this domain like others, and in what ways? How is it different from other domains, and in what ways? Recent studies reveal that the expertise necessary to successfully navigate problem-solving maps to results found in other domains, but it seems quite clear that the landscape is an "open field" at this time, when it comes to understanding the multiple interleaved goals and concerns involved with coping with complexity in this domain.

This field (like many others written about in this volume) can be seen from a dual perspective [3]. An inspiring one since people have a highly refined expertise and novel mechanisms allow to bring that expertise to bear. A worrisome one because the configuration of technology and organization is often struggling to make this expertise effective.

Looking forward, it would behoove researchers to explore this domain in greater detail. As software services continue to become more critical to society's functioning, the future depends on it.

References

1. J. Allspaw, *Trade-Offs Under Pressure: Heuristics and Observations of Teams Resolving Internet Service Outages*. M.Sc. thesis, Lund Unviversity, Sweden, 2015. Retrieved from https://lup.lub.lu.se/luur/download?func=downloadFile&recordOId=8084520&fileOId=8084521
2. J. Allspaw, Human factors and ergonomics practice in web engineering and operations: navigating a critical yet opaque sea of automation, in *Human Factors and Ergonomics in Practice* (2016), pp. 313–322
3. J. Allspaw, R.I. Cook, SRE cognitive work, in *Seeking SRE: Conversations About Running Production Systems at Scale*, ed. by D. Blank-Edelman (O'Reilly Media, 2018), pp. 441–465
4. L. Bainbridge, Ironies of automation. Automatica **19**, 775–779 (1983)
5. C. Connley, *Target Says Cash Registers Back Online and Customers Can Make Purchases Again After Systems Outage* (CNBC, 2019). Retrieved 26 May 2021, from https://www.cnbc.com/2019/06/15/targets-in-store-payment-is-system-down-impacting-stores-nationwide.html
6. E. Curran, *Work from Home to Lift Productivity by 5% in Post-pandemic U.S.* (Bloomberg, 2021). Retrieved 15 June 2021, from https://www.bloomberg.com/news/articles/2021-04-22/yes-working-from-home-makes-you-more-productive-study-finds
7. M.R. Grayson, approaching overload: diagnosis and response to Anomalies, in *Complex and Automated Production Software Systems*, ed. by D.D. Woods (The Ohio State University, 2018)
8. Z. Lanir, *Fundamental Surprise* (Decision Research, Eugene, OR, 1986)

9. L.M. Maguire, *Controlling the Costs of Coordination in Large-Scale Distributed Software Systems*. Doctoral dissertation, The Ohio State University, 2020
10. J. McCrank, *NYSE Shut Down for Nearly Four Hours by Technical Glitch* (Thomson Reuters, 2015). Retrieved from www.reuters.com/article/us-nyse-trading-idUSKCN0PI25A20150709
11. J. Mullen, *British Airways Computer Glitch Causes Big Delays at Multiple Airports* (CNNMoney, 2016). Retrieved from https://money.cnn.com/2016/09/05/news/companies/british-airways-computer-system-delays/
12. NCEES, *NCEES Discontinuing PE Software Engineering Exam* (2018). Retrieved 11 Nov 2021, from https://ncees.org/ncees-discontinuing-pe-software-engineering-exam/
13. J. Roberts, Hulu's world series stream crashed in the middle of Game 4. Fortune (2017). Retrieved 26 May 2021, from https://fortune.com/2017/10/29/world-series-hulu-crash-problems/
14. K. Schwab, More people are working remotely, and it's transforming office design. Fastcompany (2019). Retrieved 15 June 2021, from https://www.fastcompany.com/90368542/more-people-are-working-remotely-and-its-transforming-office-design
15. WKYT News Staff, *Software Issue Fixed, UK Healthcare No Longer Diverting Patients* (WKYT, 2019). Retrieved 26 May 2021, from https://www.wkyt.com/content/news/UK-HealthCare-diverting-patients-to-other-hospitals-citing-computer-issues-561140481.html

Open Access This chapter is licensed under the terms of the Creative Commons Attribution 4.0 International License (http://creativecommons.org/licenses/by/4.0/), which permits use, sharing, adaptation, distribution and reproduction in any medium or format, as long as you give appropriate credit to the original author(s) and the source, provide a link to the Creative Commons license and indicate if changes were made.

The images or other third party material in this chapter are included in the chapter's Creative Commons license, unless indicated otherwise in a credit line to the material. If material is not included in the chapter's Creative Commons license and your intended use is not permitted by statutory regulation or exceeds the permitted use, you will need to obtain permission directly from the copyright holder.

Chapter 5
Between Natural and Artificial Intelligence

Digital Sustainability in High-Risk Industries

Stian Antonsen

Abstract Algorithms have always been a key topic in safety science, whether they are governing technology through computer programming or human actors through organisational procedures. However, when the term "algorithm" is not limited to the static pre-programming of expert knowledge algorithms with the ability to change themselves, a new branch of uncertainties appears. With the concepts of epistemic uncertainty and epistemic accidents as a backdrop, I discuss safety-related challenges with the use of artificial intelligence (AI) in high-risk industries. The aim is to highlight uncertainties inherent in AI, paradoxes for safety management and risk governance, as well as the human contribution to safety in future.

Keywords Artificial intelligence · High-risk industries · Uncertainty

5.1 Introduction

Big data, algorithms and artificial intelligence (AI) are the current buzzwords in debates around technological development and how it may affect our lives, including the organisations in which we work. In this, chapter I reflects on the relationship between natural and artificial intelligence and the human contribution to safety in future.

The chapter consists of five parts. I first examine the changing division of labour between humans and technology, and the way existing safety science knowledge can be of use for future challenges. I then move on to the topic of epistemic uncertainty and epistemic accidents and concepts that I have borrowed from [5]. With Downer's concepts as sensitising devices, I turn to the way algorithms and artificial intelligence incorporate different sources of uncertainty. This includes reflections around the very concept of intelligence and the human contribution to safety in future. I conclude with the delineation of three paradoxes that need resolving before artificial intelligence can be used in high-risk industries.

S. Antonsen (✉)
NTNU Samfunnsforskning, Trondheim, Norway
e-mail: stian.antonsen@samforsk.no

© The Author(s) 2022
H. Laroche et al. (eds.), *Managing Future Challenges for Safety*,
SpringerBriefs in Safety Management,
https://doi.org/10.1007/978-3-031-07805-7_5

For readers looking for weaknesses, I can be of assistance by highlighting a limitation that should be borne in mind when reading the text. Being a sociologist means that if I were to inspect the programming of complex algorithms, I would have a hard time understanding what I am looking at—I simply don't know the language it is built in. However, this is part of the well-known challenge of *explainability*—the ability of algorithmic systems and programming languages to facilitate not only communication of computations to physical computers, but to human beings, allowing them to understand, scrutinise and criticise as we do with any other text [3]. Nevertheless, the sociologist's perspective means that the discussion is restricted to the *logic* of algorithms, the uncertainties associated with algorithms and the role of humans in an algorithmic world.

5.2 The Changing Nature of Work

Algorithms have always been a key topic for the design of safe and reliable sociotechnical systems. Broadly speaking, an algorithm is a finite set of rules aiming to govern actions on the form of "if this happens, in this context, then conduct these actions, in this sequence". On the technology side, automated safety systems (e.g. emergency shutdown systems) are indispensable for controlling hazardous energy. They consist of computer-programmed rules for actions taken by technology, e.g. "if this set of criteria is satisfied, then do the following actions to shut down this list of systems". On the organisational side, standard operation procedures follow the same logic, albeit with different challenges regarding compliance to the predefined instructions: "If an operator opens a valve in a pressurised system, then open gradually at 5, 20 and 50% before fully opening the valve". Hence, algorithms are already everywhere but as high-risk systems are digitalised and more real-time data becomes available, the use of complex algorithms will be a key topic for safety management in the years to come.

Increased use of algorithms involves a change in the division of labour between humans and technology. There is a myriad of classifications in this domain [10, 13], but they all have to do with the allocation of functions and decision-making authority between humans and technology, usually along an axis between fully manual and fully automated operations. While the taxonomies are simplifications, rarely distinguishing between different modes of operation (e.g. normal operation vs. unforeseen situations), they provide a backdrop for distinguishing between different uses of algorithms.

Such classifications are well-known within cognitive ergonomics, giving rise to concerns regarding human-in-the-loop issues, e.g. challenges to situation awareness, deskilling or automation failures [6]. The crash of AF447 in 2009 illustrates the human-in-the-loop paradox: inconsistent speed readings made the autopilot disconnect, immediately changing the aircraft from a highly automated system to a highly manual system, at an altitude where pilots rarely fly manually [9]. The assumption behind this sudden transfer of tasks and decision-making from technology to humans is that the human pilots will be ready to take over in a split second. Ready in terms of manual flying skills, training and situation awareness. It is such assumptions and expectations inscribed in technology that I will be discussing in this chapter.

One sometimes gets the feeling that classifications of the division of labour between humans and technology are treated as maturity scales that systems are inevitably moving and even *should* be moving from left to right on the scale. It seems to have become common knowledge that the information processing capabilities of "artificial intelligence" (AI) far surpass the capacity of human intelligence and that decisions and actions should, therefore, be transferred from humans to technology to reduce the occurrence of human error. While this assertion may be valid when referring to algorithm-based tools used in stable contexts, the presence of major accident potential and a high level of variability makes this more problematic. Scales describing the division of labour between humans and technology should, therefore, be treated as a lens for the design of tasks and responsibilities within sociotechnical systems, considering where it may be wise to use some form of automation and where human capabilities outshine those of technology. This is by no means a new question for safety science, meaning that many of the lessons from the past are relevant for the challenges of the future.

However, when the term "algorithm" not only refers to the static pre-programming of expert knowledge but includes the ability for systems to change themselves and communicate autonomously with other technological actors, a new branch of challenges and uncertainties appears. This is where algorithms become far more than rules automating simple actions and recurring decisions, relieving human beings of routine tasks. They are no longer only replacing human actions; they are touted as alternatives to human *intelligence*. This raises a different set of questions—questions related to uncertainty. Uncertainty here refers to the way technology is always based on incomplete knowledge and assumptions. As these assumptions can never be fully tested, they will be sources of inevitable surprises as a system operates over time [5].

5.3 Uncertainty and Epistemic Accidents

The works of Downer [4, 5] are important when it comes to safety-related challenges in algorithms and AI. Drawing on perspectives from Science and Technology Studies, Downer sheds light on the way assumptions about reality are built into technology, models, tests and verification. This is a particular form of uncertainty, arising from assumptions about the world in which a piece of technology is going to operate, assumptions which can never be fully representative of the world. This forms the basis of a particular form of accidents, which he calls epistemic accidents.

Epistemic accidents are the results of specific events revealing holes in the knowledge underlying the tests and models devised to represent real-life operational contexts. [5, p. 83]

The point is that technology cannot be seen in isolation from the knowledge on which their design is based—assumptions about everything from material fatigue, the needed strength of physical barriers or the way a piece of software should work under different operating conditions. These assumptions cannot be tested in an experimental environment that is representative of all possible contextual variability in the reality in which the systems are put to work. This means that the success of ultra-safe systems like aviation is not only due to technology being tested in simulators and laboratories, but that part of the success comes from learning the hard way—through a history of disasters [5]. This raises some tricky questions about "residual risk" which are hard to speak about, both politically and ethically, but which are important issues to raise around the use of algorithms and AI in high-risk systems.

5.4 Assumptions and Uncertainty in Artificial Intelligence

Keeping Downer's concepts in mind when moving on to algorithms involved in AI, there is an obvious need to say something about the term AI. As is the case with the general concept of intelligence, the definition and understanding of artificial intelligence is contested [7]. For this discussion, a broad definition will suffice. I see AI as referring to any kind of computing technology that aims to mimic or otherwise resemble human intelligence. According to Boucher [2], existing AI technology can be divided into two waves. The first wave consists of "good old-fashioned AI" based on precise rules that are the encoding of human knowledge in contexts where there is little variability and where it is possible to specify right and wrong solutions by means of strict "if–then–else" rules.[1] While the first wave is human-driven, the second wave is data-driven in the sense that it consists of various forms of machine learning (ML). In ML, the learning does not consist only of humans refining the rules (algorithms) to improve performance but includes an ability to improve the fit of the rules through identified patterns in large quantities of data. This is where the terms "artificial neural networks" and "deep learning" (referring to artificial neural networks with at least two hidden layers) come in.

As the aim of the chapter is to discuss the logic of AI for use in high-risk domains, I will not go into the details of the techniques in question. Instead, I will delineate key steps in developing and modifying AI to show that the algorithms not only incorporate epistemic uncertainty into the systems stemming from the assumptions of its creator—it may also produce brand new uncertainties based on their own assumptions. My argument is that there is a form of epistemic uncertainty built into models and algorithms that gain a form of objectivity because they are seemingly untouched by human fallibility of judgement, while in fact they are not.

---

[1] This includes both systems where each variable has an absolute value true (1) or false (0), and systems based on fuzzy logic allowing any value between 0 and 1.

Let's take an example from supervised machine learning. Say we want to create an algorithm able to separate criminals from non-criminals based on images, a project carried out in 2016 [1].

The first thing we need is an existing data set consisting of images of *known* criminals and non-criminals. Since we already know who are criminals and non-criminals, we can label each picture accordingly, thereby providing the system with enough cues to allow a learning algorithm to be run. The system is sent looking for patterns in the pictures, singling out recurring differences in the labelled data. The learning algorithm has now created a programme where it knows what to look for—which markers in the images that explain the most variance in the data. Now comes the crucial step: exposing the programme to new data which it has never seen before. Its creator hopes it will make correct predictions when sorting the test data into the two labels (criminals vs. non-criminals). As the process goes on and the software gets feedback on its performance, the programme will change to improve its fit, based on how the learning algorithm is set up.

Where are the possible sources of uncertainty? Starting with the selection of training data and labelling—where are the images found, and how do you know how to label them? To know someone is a criminal, you will need police information. Which images do you select of them? And how do you know that someone that is *not convicted* of anything is not a criminal? Add gender, race, clothing style, etc. to the selection criteria, and things get complicated both in terms of data selection, fairness and ethics. In the case in question, the algorithm basically learned to separate people smiling from the ones not smiling, since they used photographs of criminals taken by the police and ordinary pictures of happy people on the non-criminal side [1].

Moving to the learning algorithm—what is the algorithm going to pay attention to in the pixels of the images of criminals and non-criminals? In supervised machine learning, it will need guidance—colour, contrast, background, angles between nose and lips, cheek bones, etc. In unsupervised learning, it will create these patterns itself. In any case, it will be a selection, and this will be a process worth considering in terms of understanding what it is doing and why.

Moving on to the test data, this is where things really get messy. This is when the programme is faced with data it has never seen before and tries to classify new observations based on what it has learned from the training data. In the example of recognising criminals, it will be given more data, with more variation and encounter far more problems. To predict whether a person is in fact a criminal, the system will need a model ranking the observations according to several scales and a line dividing the criminals from the non-criminals. This is, in fact, a form of generalisation, drawing lessons from experience to something it has never seen before. There are numerous examples showing that this is very challenging, even in presumably simple image recognition like the reading of handwriting on envelopes in the postal services [1]. A final point is the lack of transparency as to what the software actually looks like once it has run for a while and changed its criteria for classification—who is able to verify what the programme is doing, and which assumptions it has created for its own classifications?

The example is about image recognition and not safety–critical decision-making. What does this tell us about algorithms in safety–critical planning, management and operations? First of all, it provides a general warning that algorithms are never neutral. Algorithms will reflect the shortcomings in knowledge of their creators, and no matter how brilliant the test data, there is no way of escaping the uncertain assumptions about the world underlying their working. Whether these assumptions stem from the algorithm's creator or from its ability to change itself, they will still be uncertain.

But, there are even simpler questions to ask concerning data—both the training and test data. The most obvious question is whether there is *enough* data. In terms of monitoring the technical condition of equipment, there might be enough data to do this. This might replace manual human work by providing predictive recommendations for maintenance and replacement, as long as there is no need for professional and contextual judgement. But, these are routine tasks that are repeated over and over. If we are talking about the more complex tasks that human operators do, that have a more situational component of judgement, it is much harder to see where one would find the data able to match the choices made with the situational characteristics that make them meaningful.

Another question is how these data become available for analysis in the first place. A disproportionate share of attention and resources within computer science is devoted to analysis methods, treating the input data as pre-existing objects [11]. Data is rarely "discovered" as objective facts and analysed as such—it is both selected and prepared before it is available for analysis (ibid.). This is a more serious challenge than the well-known potential for "garbage in, garbage out". It points, again, to the invisible production of uncertainties, only that it provides both data and algorithms with a form of misplaced objectivity that only becomes visible after some kind of failure.

In safety–critical contexts, we cannot afford to overlook the fact that data will be biased, labelling contains bias, and that learning algorithms can create their own set of bias. Therefore, there is no reason to believe that AI removes human fallibility. It replaces one form of human fallibility with another.

5.5 The Human Contribution to Safety in Future

It follows from the discussion so far that the human contribution to safety will be a topic for safety science in future, although our study of it may require additions to our theoretical repertoire. One of the questions in the workshop from which this book arises was "what forms can the human contribution to safety take in future?" When reflecting on this question, I realised that I am not that worried that humans will be made obsolete by artificial intelligence anytime soon. While the automation of routine actions and decisions that has been ongoing since the industrial revolution is not likely to come to a halt, safety–critical sensemaking may be one of the last instances where humans could be replaced. And the reason for this is that our intelligence is *not* artificial. I will try to explain my argument by reflecting on what intelligence can be.

The concept of intelligence is contested and multifaceted. It has been used to refer to numerous behaviours linked to some form of performance, but where the performance cannot be separated from its specific contexts [12]. The point here is not to go into detail on the concept of intelligence, but it is worthwhile considering what we mean by the term when we discuss the relationship between human and artificial intelligence. This includes a consideration of the contexts where intelligence is regarded as key to successful performance, for which tasks which form of intelligence is beneficial and the difference between artificial and natural intelligence in this respect.

Specialised, narrow intelligence is the first form. This means mastering very specific tasks to perfection, but the capabilities are limited to that particular task. This is what Google Assistant does. It masters the translation from voice commands to tasks like an internet search or turning an electrical appliance on and off. This kind of AI is everywhere. It is impressive and cool, and it keeps improving. But, it can only apply intelligence to the specific problems for which it is programmed. All it can do is basically search the internet faster and more comprehensively than an individual can. Google Assistant and Siri are little more than natural language processing algorithms used together with predefined rules.

Physical intelligence is another category and is derived through physical and practiced learning. Sports, dancing or craftsmanship is common examples. When you think about it, these are complex skills because they link aspects of the mind with the motor skills of the body. Robots that are able to run on uneven terrain or ride a bicycle have been around for more than a decade, impressing the audience with their ability to perform (well, almost) human-like movements based on a triangulation of data across a number of sensors. But, my guess is that the development of these robots has taken years and millions of dollars, while your average 6-year-old child can learn it intuitively in a day or two. This gives the human contribution to safety a continued role in future—while our information processing capacity in narrow domains may be limited, our action repertoire in the physical world is not particularly limited, since we can improvise with whatever tools and information we have at hand.

The last category is general, common-sense intelligence. This is probably what we have in mind when we use the term intelligence—the ability to interpret and understand virtually any situation and learn how to act in that situation. This includes understanding cause and effect. AI can understand that two observations are correlated, but it is still more or less clueless when it comes to causality. A statistical model can establish a correlation between clouds and rain and make good predictions about the probability of rain, but it has no idea what a cloud is. Translated to the domain of safety, the model may be able to rank different decision and action alternatives according to the labelled severity of consequences, but it has no understanding about accidents or death. The same reasoning goes for a human's contextual understanding of a social situation and the ability to pick up subtle cues from its environment, even though it has never been in a similar situation before. This is one of the key human contributions to safety. Common-sense knowledge, along with professional judgement, is what make humans capable of sensemaking. Humans are able to make good guesses in rare situations, based on incomplete information. In the field of AI, common-sense intelligence has simply not been invented yet.

The point of these reflections is that when we say that AI has superior information processing capacity compared to humans, this is only partly right. It can apply some form of intelligence in the form of information processing on *narrowly defined areas, where there is sufficient data and the similar situations occur over and over again*. It can also beat humans at chess or Alpha Go, but this is based on the computer being faster and better at calculating and simulating a wide range of different game scenarios. And make no mistake, this is a fantastic skill. However, we are only comparing a small part of the intelligence repertoire and the one aspect where AI currently has an edge. It is somewhat of a paradox that comparisons between human and artificial intelligence seem to be based on the premises of what artificial intelligence is capable of, not what human intelligence is capable of.

As follows from the previous sections, the human contribution to safety is more than standardised information processing around narrowly defined tasks. In most other aspects of intelligence, artificial intelligence does not even come close. This is where the buzz around AI is ridiculously hyped and mystified. In its current stage of development, AI is software written to do specific tasks. It is not alive, it does not have a consciousness, and it is completely incapable of understanding, creativity and empathy [2]. This is important to stress, because both the promises and worries sometimes seem to be aimed at technology which has not yet been invented.

5.6 Implications—The Future of Risk

Summing up these considerations, there are several paradoxes involved in the use of algorithms and AI in safety–critical settings. These are paradoxes that will need some form of resolution before AI is put into use in safety–critical decision-making.

First is what we can call an intelligence paradox. It consists of two branches where the first is associated with the access to and selection of training data. Intelligence requires experience. If there is "garbage in, garbage out" in training data, it might be artificial, but it is not intelligence. The other branch has to do with the kind of intelligence needed in different circumstances in high-risk industries and the human contribution in this respect. As long as general AI simply does not exist, the drive towards reducing the human contribution in high-risk settings should not only be a question of *how*, but a question of *why*. Answering this question should not only focus on the narrow capabilities of artificial intelligence but the general capabilities of human intelligence.

Second is a transparency paradox. When algorithms learn, they become *actors* in safety management. It is a basic principle of HROs and most advice on safety management that important decisions and actions must be checked and double-checked. Assigning a critical task or decision to technology does not revoke this need. If it is hard to qualify technological actors' interpretations and assumptions, it is a breach of basic principles of redundancy and accountability.

Third is what I call a verification paradox. It is a variant of the transparency paradox, but the third one has more to do with the long-term follow up of learning algorithms. I think, or at least hope, that regulators and supervisory authorities will never allow critical decision-making processes to change unsupervised. The governance of self-learning algorithms requires regulation, audit tools and competence, something which is not in place, and it is hard to see how this can be done, at least within a prescriptive regulatory regime. The matter of verification also touches upon the larger problematics of bias, ethics and fairness of AI systems [8], which is also likely to be of great importance for safety science.

High-risk industries are moving into a landscape where software becomes more safety–critical than before, making software engineers more critical than before. It is not a wild guess that the patterns of failure will change, from traditional operator (human) errors to more software-related (human) errors. This includes the possibility for algorithmic surprise. If tests and simulation are by definition incomplete (remember Downer's argument), surprises will occur. Trial and error will persist as a prerequisite for learning, possibly creating some very unpleasant situations for both companies and regulators. As algorithms and AI enter the field of human factors, we should rethink the way we conceptualise and study the relationship between the human and technological agent of safety. The need for human factors expertise is probably more relevant in the age of artificial intelligence than it has ever been before.

Acknowledgement The chapter is published as part of the project Theoretical Advances of Cyber Resilience (TECNOCRACI), funded by the Research Council of Norway through grant no. 303489.

References

1. C.T. Bergstrom, J.D. West, *Calling Bullshit. The Art of Skepticism in a Data-Driven World* (Penguin Random House, New York, 2020)
2. P. Boucher, *How Artificial Intelligence Works* (European Parliament, 2019). Retrieved from https://www.europarl.europa.eu/RegData/etudes/BRIE/2019/634420/EPRS_BRI(2019)634420_EN.pdf
3. S. Dasgupta, *Computer Science: A Very Short Introduction* (Oxford University Press, Oxford, 2016)
4. J. Downer, "737-cabriolet": the limits of knowledge and the sociology of inevitable failure. Am. J. Sociol. **117**(3), 725–762 (2011)
5. J. Downer, On ignorance and apocalypse: a brief introduction to "epistemic accidents", in *Safety Science Research: Evolution, Challenges and New Directions*, ed. by J.-C. Le Coze (CRC Press, Boca Raton, 2020)
6. J. Hoc, From human-machine interaction to human-machine cooperation. Ergonomics **43**(7), 833–843 (2000). https://doi.org/10.1080/001401300409044
7. S. Legg, M. Hutter, A collection of definitions of intelligence. Front. Artif. Intell. Appl. **157**, 17–24 (2007)
8. N. Mehrabi, F. Morstatter, N. Saxena, K. Lerman, A. Galstyan, A Survey on Bias and Fairness in Machine Learning (2019). Retrieved from ArXivabs/1908.09635

9. N. Oliver, T. Calvard, K. Potočnik, Cognition, technology, and organizational limits: lessons from the Air France 447 disaster. Organ. Sci. **28**(4), 729–743 (2017)
10. R. Parasuraman, T.B. Sheridan, A model for types and levels of human interaction with automation. Syst. Man Cybern. **30**(3), 286–297 (2000)
11. E. Parmiggiani, T. Østerlie, P. Almklov, In the backrooms of data science. J. Assoc. Inf. Syst. **23**(1), 139–164 (2022)
12. H.D. Schlinger, The myth of intelligence. Psychol. Rec. **53**(1), 15–32 (2003)
13. T.B. Sheridan, W.L. Verplanck, *Human and Computer control of Undersea Teleoperators* (MIT Man–Machine Systems Laboratory Report, MIT, Cambridge, MA, 1978)

Open Access This chapter is licensed under the terms of the Creative Commons Attribution 4.0 International License (http://creativecommons.org/licenses/by/4.0/), which permits use, sharing, adaptation, distribution and reproduction in any medium or format, as long as you give appropriate credit to the original author(s) and the source, provide a link to the Creative Commons license and indicate if changes were made.

The images or other third party material in this chapter are included in the chapter's Creative Commons license, unless indicated otherwise in a credit line to the material. If material is not included in the chapter's Creative Commons license and your intended use is not permitted by statutory regulation or exceeds the permitted use, you will need to obtain permission directly from the copyright holder.

Chapter 6
Careers Surpassing a Half-Century: A Look at Japan and France

Or How Should the Issues Associated with Long Careers and Their Impact on Safety Be Managed?

Akira Tose and Dounia Tazi

Abstract In Japan, population ageing is leading the government to raise the retirement age to beyond 70, and even to 75 by 2040. This policy of maintaining older workers in employment is compelling companies to provide job opportunities to people with up to 50 years of work experience. This has consequences on the updating of skills—particularly, those related to new technologies, on employee engagement and motivation, on the management of age-related constraints in workstation ergonomics and work organisation, and it could pose a serious threat to safety. This chapter aims to describe the situation in Japan and the possible solutions put forward to overcome challenges. It then invites reflection on the management of longer careers in France and in Europe, where population projections also point to an increasingly aged population by 2040.

Keywords Ageing workforce · Skills management · Safety culture

6.1 The Situation in Japan: A Possible Projection of What the Future Situation Will Be in Europe and France

Population ageing is a major issue in Japan, which has the highest old-age dependency ratio of all OECD countries (over 50 persons aged 65 and above for every 100 persons aged 20–64 in 2017, ratio that is projected to rise to 79/100 in 2050) [3]. The Japanese government is asking the industrial sector to offer employment opportunities to older people, with a target of 70 years old from 2021. Forecasts predict that this age will rise to 75 by 2040. Currently in Japan, over 30% of men and 20% of women aged 70–74 are employed in a professional occupation. It is predicted that the labour force

A. Tose (✉)
Niigata University, Niigata, Japan
e-mail: tose@eng.niigata-u.ac.jp

D. Tazi
Icsi, Toulouse, France

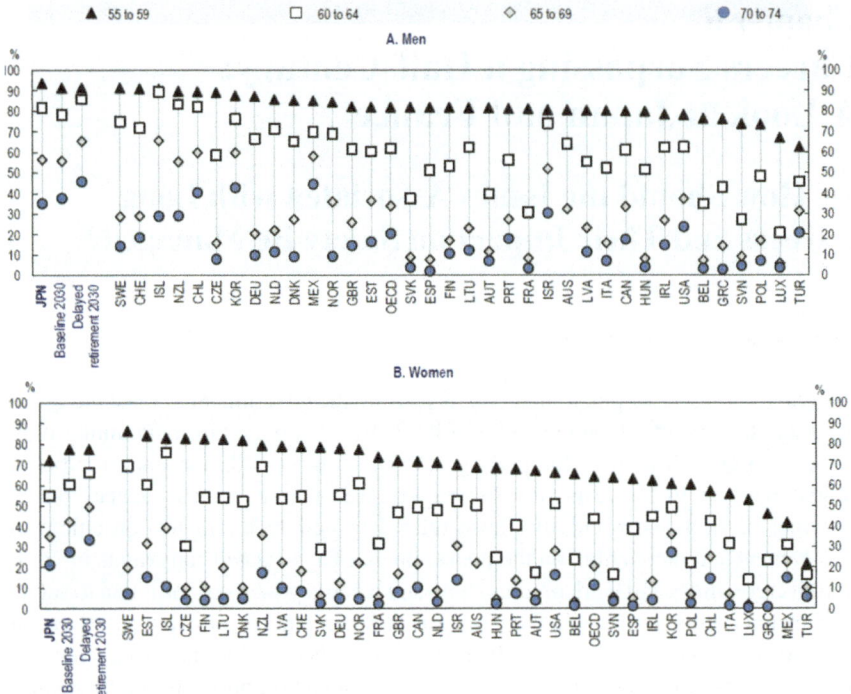

Fig. 6.1 Percentage of the population in the labour force in each age group in OECD countries in 2017 (and 2030 for Japan). Reproduced from [3] with permission; all rights reserved

participation rate in this portion of the population will continue to increase over the next ten years [3] (Fig. 6.1).

In Europe, there are many disparities in the legal retirement age. The average is 65 years old. In France, the legal age for retirement is 62, and discussions are ongoing to raise this to 64. In 2020, the average retirement age in France was 62.8 years old [1].

6.2 Careers Surpassing a Half-Century: The Main Challenges

What will happen if the career span of all workers surpasses 50 years? Organisational "sclerosis" due to a predominance of the most experienced—but also the oldest—employees in the most senior positions; a drop in employee motivation; constraints and limitations associated with biological ageing; a reduced capacity for innovation… Raising the retirement age without any real strategy causes serious problems in companies and could have an impact on safety.

Following are some of the main challenges that Japanese companies are already facing:

- skills and knowledge updating and the opportunity to offer training or retraining possibilities throughout a person's career;
- managing the mix of generations: generations of grandfather, father and grandson working for a same company;
- the ability to offer rewarding positions to the most experienced employees, but not necessarily in senior management;
- ergonomics, and more generally taking into account human factors, whether in the design of workstations or the work organisation, in order to accommodate the mix of generations.

6.3 What Strategies Can Be Used to Manage This Situation? A Few Examples Being Tested in Japan

6.3.1 Giving Employees the Possibility of Updating Their Skills and Knowledge Throughout Their Career

Skills and knowledge updating throughout an employee's career seem to be an option favoured in Japan. This updating is in several areas: technical skills, managerial skills, interpersonal and communication skills. Major changes are also occurring in instructional methods and ways of learning, with more emphasis being placed on flipped learning, or in other words doing the conceptual learning remotely and using attendance time to practise applying the skills. Other instructional methods are favoured such as simulation, mentoring or the buddy system and on-the-job coaching. These changes have an impact on both the trainees and the trainers.

In high-risk companies, it seems important to have the most experienced people contribute to keeping alive the memory of the most serious accidents, which are becoming less and less frequent. However, there should be clear guidelines as to which safety best practices they can share. After all, certain practices which were acceptable a few years ago may not be so today. Thus, it seems necessary to provide a selection of safety best practices to perpetuate. Integrating the consideration of human and organisational factors in professional training and development programmes also appears to be increasingly important in the field of safety. For management, this takes the form of courses on safety leadership.

To avoid organisational "sclerosis" potentially brought on by a predominance of the most experienced people in senior management positions, Japan is exploring what the right timing and pace might be for undertaking this intensive updating of skills. This exploration includes the retraining of the most experienced workers (Table 6.1).

Table 6.1 Example of an intensive training offering in a future company

Age	Content and objective of the professional development
Around 30–40 years old	Preparation for being a good manager/professional engineer • Safety management • Managerial skills • Interpersonal skills and human and organisational factors
Around 50–60 years old	Preparation for new long-career opportunities • Updating of management and safety knowledge • Training in new instructional techniques, communication, consulting to train or support the younger generations • Finding new retraining opportunities

6.3.2 Managing the Mix of Generations

In Japan, it is relatively common for a generation of grandfather, son and grandson to be working for the same company. Companies must, therefore, manage this mix of generations which can create tensions, particularly when the grandfather generation monopolises the senior management positions.

It is indeed customary to offer the management and executive positions to the most experienced people, i.e. those in the 60–70 age group. However, if all these positions are held by the most experienced people, this considerably limits opportunities for the next generation, in the 50–60 age bracket, to advance to these positions. Although they will be senior in terms of skills, they will not be allowed to access such managerial functions. This situation could lead companies to limit the hiring of young workers and cause the 50–60 generation and the next to leave the organisation or to lose motivation due to the lack of prospects. There is a risk of organisational "sclerosis", which could affect these companies' capacity for innovation.

Moreover, the backgrounds, training, expectations vis-à-vis the company and even the values of the different generations working together can differ. The company must manage this diversity.

6.3.3 Offering Rewarding Positions to the Most Experienced

Japan is experimenting with different ways to offer people rewarding positions without raising their salary or offering senior management positions to the workers with the most experience.

Three types of positions or retraining possibilities are currently being tested for the oldest people:

- on-site trainer or coach;
- technical expert;
- independent consultant.

For the most experienced people to be placed in an on-site trainer or coach position, they must learn new teaching and coaching skills, decisions must be made regarding the practices to be taught, and workstation ergonomics must be adapted.

If they are to be placed in positions as technical experts, they require access to training and continuous professional development in order to regularly update their technical and interpersonal skills. And lastly, positioning these experienced people as independent consultants implies managing their exit from the company and requires them to have the ability to make the shift from manager to consultant and accept this change in status.

6.3.4 Ergonomics and Consideration of Human and Organisational Factors

The concomitance of several generations within a same company requires rethinking workstation ergonomics to adapt to the needs and limitations of each individual. In addition to workstation ergonomics, this mix has an impact on work organisation overall, whether in terms of physical elements such as workspace management—since, for example, the most experienced people are attached to having their own office, or in terms of work schedule or even of managing telecommuting or blended working, for example [2].

6.4 Discussion

These elements from Japan should prompt a reflection in France and Europe on the management of long careers and their potential impact on safety.

Three questions arise directly from the reflections and experiments undertaken in Japan on how to design a professional development programme that spans the entire career in order to improve the management of safety and the prevention of major accidents.

- What might constitute a "rewarding position" for the most experienced employees?
- What types of professional experience or skills and knowledge development might be needed to offer older employees these "rewarding positions"?
- How can the norms governing work design and organisation be changed to ensure safe operations while integrating the mix of generations within companies?

Two additional questions should also be considered in order to investigate the impact on safety and are discussed below.

6.4.1 Age Limit and Safety

Given the biological laws of ageing, are there any professions in which a lower age limit should be imposed for the sake of safety?

Indeed, the decline in cognitive and psychomotor performance and the higher risk of incapacity or sudden death (that come with ageing) could lead to a person becoming unsuitable for their role. Some frontline operator professions come to mind, such as airline pilot, nuclear power reactor operator, air traffic controller, train driver or surgeon. The literature on the ageing of airline pilots shows that it is very difficult to determine an age limit, because (1) the effects of ageing differ widely between individuals, and (2) by drawing on their experience, these operators develop compensatory strategies which allow them to perform their tasks very satisfactorily despite a significant decline in cognitive function measured separately from their occupation. Thus, the practical outcome in aviation depends on the economic situation: when there are too many pilots, impairment due to ageing is invoked in order to oblige pilots to retire, whereas when more pilots are needed, the justification mentioned above is invoked to keep anyone whom medical and professional bodies deem still fit to fly [4].

6.4.2 Generational Mix and Safety

What harmonious local and contextual generational mix, what balanced local and contextual age pyramid would enable a better management of the impact of long careers on safety?

Economic considerations are pushing the retirement age upwards, but the established general rule then applies to age pyramids that are possibly very different from one company to the next. Yet, when it comes to safety, what matters within a company is to have a balanced ecosystem with a harmonious intergenerational mix and above all to avoid retiring large numbers of highly experienced employees at a time and then massively replacing them with inexperienced young people without having some kind of process in place for the transmission of empirical knowledge. This type of "mass replacement" may prove more acceptable or even advisable in future, with rapid and frequent technological changes giving youth a growing advantage. However, the knowledge required to manage the safety of increasingly complex systems will not be limited to the most recent technical component. Therefore, a balance must be struck between the interests of productivity and economic performance and those of safety. Moreover, in addition to being specific to each company, the age pyramid also depends on the past and current attractiveness of the particular industry.

More than the "usability" of older workers, what should be worked on is the attractiveness, the distribution and maintaining employability across the entire age pyramid. This would imply managing retirement ages differently according not only to the occupation, the harshness of its working conditions and its relationship to risk, but also according to the company, the age pyramids, etc.

References

1. CNAV, *Statistiques, recherches et prospective de la Caisse Nationale d'Assurance Vieillesse* (2021). Retrieved from CNAV Retraite & Action Sociale: https://www.statistiques-recherches.cnav.fr/age-de-depart-a-la-retraite.html
2. J. Martine, J. Jaussaud, Prolonging working life in Japan: issues and practices for elderly employment in an aging society. Contemp. Jpn. **30**(2), 227–242 (2018). https://doi.org/10.1080/18692729.2018.1504530
3. OECD, Working better with age: Japan, in *Ageing and Employment Policies* (OECD, Paris, 2018). https://doi.org/10.1787/9789264201996-en
4. P.S. Tsang, Assessing cognitive aging in piloting, in *Human Error in Aviation* (Routledge, 2017), pp. 425–464

Open Access This chapter is licensed under the terms of the Creative Commons Attribution 4.0 International License (http://creativecommons.org/licenses/by/4.0/), which permits use, sharing, adaptation, distribution and reproduction in any medium or format, as long as you give appropriate credit to the original author(s) and the source, provide a link to the Creative Commons license and indicate if changes were made.

The images or other third party material in this chapter are included in the chapter's Creative Commons license, unless indicated otherwise in a credit line to the material. If material is not included in the chapter's Creative Commons license and your intended use is not permitted by statutory regulation or exceeds the permitted use, you will need to obtain permission directly from the copyright holder.

Chapter 7
Senior Mentoring, Skills Transfer Subject to Conditions

Tania Navarro Rodríguez and Alexandre Largier

Abstract The purpose of this chapter is to highlight the main findings of French language studies on senior mentoring. It shows in particular that mentoring is a protean system which can be defined and fashioned by the way it is exercised, by the type of activity that it involves and by the context in which the mentoring practices take place.

Keywords Mentoring · Skill transfer · Seniors

7.1 Introduction

Although much debated, the involvement of seniors in mentoring has aroused the interest of manufacturers, the government and researchers in France for several years, as demonstrated by the "Masingue" government report published in 2009 on senior mentoring, the consideration given to this issue in risk industries, in particular the nuclear industry, as well as the numerous publications dedicated to this subject in the human and social sciences (sociology, education sciences, management sciences, etc.). All these players seem to share the same concern: mentoring, and in particular senior mentoring, is considered to be the most appropriate solution to solve the problem of skill transfer.

Recent French language studies have analysed how seniors develop transverse mentoring skills [4]. Other studies have explored how to enhance company mentoring, demonstrating in particular that mentoring is "partner-based teaching, which commits the company collectively" [5]. Lastly, some studies have focused on the deployment of mentoring [6], placing the emphasis on certain limitations in the implementation of senior mentoring.

This document puts in perspective some data drawn from French language literature dedicated to senior mentoring. We will try to identify certain questions that

---

T. N. Rodríguez (✉) · A. Largier
IRSN, Fontenay-aux-Roses, France
e-mail: tania.navarrorodriguez@irsn.fr

need to be answered concerning the implementation of senior mentoring. Although mentoring can be defined

> as a teaching approach based on a guided work situation [and a] professional socialization instrument. [5, p. 24]

it nevertheless remains a protean system. It seems useful to investigate the way it is exercised, the type of activity and the context in which the mentoring practices take place.

7.2 Mentoring, Numerous Forms and Varied Contexts

Mentoring may aim to reproduce practices or anticipate changes [8]. The extent to which company mentoring is formalised also contributes to the definition and organisation of mentoring: implementation or not of training for the mentors to prepare them for their roles; implementation or not of means, times and places giving mentors the opportunity to examine their practices. According to B. Masingue, there are numerous types of mentoring: traditional mentoring, cross-mentoring, reverse mentoring, expert mentoring, hierarchical mentoring. All these types can be organised in different ways: tandem or collective; fixed or rotating; organised around a team whose members act as mentors on a segment of their activity, or performed by employees working full-time as mentors. Similarly, mentoring can be organised for a given group of jobs or on a cross-company basis. Lastly, the company context must also be considered: depending on its stability and the need to adapt rapidly, mentoring will be more or less appropriate [7].

Some informal mentoring practices have existed for many years, and the skills transmitted on this occasion may extend far beyond the purely technical aspect of the activity. Representations of the profession, the management, the organisation may also be transmitted, as well as local values and standards, etc., which may sometimes conflict with other company messages. In some configurations, the implementation of "institutional" mentoring may destabilise existing practices which have stood the test of time, in particular as regards safety, with for example the transmission of prudence know-how [2].

In his analysis of company mentoring operating modes, [8] demonstrates that this function is often poorly formalised, the mentor's activities not being precisely defined. In this case, it often consists of informal actions obeying a training logic in a work situation. According to this author, mentoring practices cover several broad types of activity, in particular: induction of new hires aiming to integrate them into a project and to give a presentation of the company entities; explanation of the work and day-to-day follow-up; assessment of the results, which is often poorly formalised (spontaneous assessment). For all these reasons, evaluating the effects of mentoring proves difficult [3].

7.3 Seniors, All Mentors

The assumption that seniors are the best placed and the most able to act as mentors has been questioned by the Masingue report:

> The idea that mentors would obviously be seniors and that seniors are automatically good mentors must be seriously put into perspective in view of the facts. It would even represent a "false truth". [7, p. 5]

Firstly, acting as a mentor is not purely a matter of possessing high technical skills. The mentor must also possess basic teaching skills and must be willing to be a mentor. Transmission does not simply consist in "pouring" a skill into a container—the mentee. Mentoring is a teaching–learning relationship which, to be effective, feeds on discussions, questioning and professional arguments [1]. The mentoring activity therefore involves listening, reformulation, stimulation and reflection regarding the role-play conditions.

In addition, the mentoring activity also affects the mentor. Mentoring cannot just be considered as a simple one-way transfer of skills from the mentor to the mentee. This practice has a retroactive effect on mentors. These effects of mentorship on the mentors themselves are generally not perceived by organisations. The practices may be explained by reflection–action situations at work: development of the ability to consider and analyse situations and practices (transverse skill transferable to other situations) and development of a critical eye on oneself, one's practices and one's own ability to act by taking a detached look at the action (meta-skill: ability to look at one's own skills and means of action). Wittorski indicates that mentoring may lead the mentor to produce a critical distancing approach [8, p. 22].

This is because this attitude promotes a reflexive position and because the new hire is also a source of enrichment for the mentor. For these two reasons, mentors may have to change their practices, positions and representations, a situation which may be badly received when not chosen freely.

In addition, in some activities, seniors are not necessarily the best placed to perform mentoring activities. This is especially true in activities where knowledge quickly becomes obsolete, for example sales activities where the products change rapidly, and activities in which the technical devices used are being constantly upgraded. This may also be the case of highly arduous activities in which the community (and the organisation) may choose to "preserve" the seniors by keeping them away from the field and by assigning them administrative, preparation or site monitoring tasks, for example.

Lastly, in some organisations with rapid job turnover, a senior in the company, even with extensive general experience, may be a relative newcomer to their job. And to think that a senior is familiar with the field just because they worked in it 20 years ago may prove dangerous since, frequently, everything has moved on since then.

References

1. Y. Clot, Réhabiliter la dispute professionnelle. Le journal de l'école de Paris du management **1**, 9–16 (2014)
2. D. Cru, Les savoir-faire de prudence: un enjeu pour la prévention. Consignes formelles et pratiques informelles de sécurité, in *Les risques du travail*, ed. by A. Thébaud-Mony, P. Davezies, L. Vogel, S. Volkoff (La Découverte, Paris, 2015)
3. C. Delgoulet, A. Largier, G. Tirilly, La mesure des tutorats en entreprise: enjeux, complexité et limites. Form. Empl. (124), 45–62 (2013)
4. L. Durat, Former des retraités au tutorat: questionner les incidents critiques pour conceptualiser les compétences transversales liées à l'action. Recherches en éducation (42), 169–198 (2020)
5. A. Fredy-Planchot, Reconnaître le tutorat en entreprise. Rev. Fr. Gest. **6**(175), 23–32 (2007)
6. D. Laport, Le tutorat intergénérationnel, l'épreuve de la preuve. Pensée plurielle **3**(40), 73–84 (2015)
7. B. Masingue, *Seniors tuteurs: comment faire mieux?* (Rapport au Secrétaire d'État chargé de l'Emploi, Ministère du travail, de l'emploi et de l'insertion, 2009)
8. R. Wittorski, Évolution des compétences professionnelles des tuteurs par l'exercice du tutorat. Rech. Form. (22), 35–46 (1996)

Open Access This chapter is licensed under the terms of the Creative Commons Attribution 4.0 International License (http://creativecommons.org/licenses/by/4.0/), which permits use, sharing, adaptation, distribution and reproduction in any medium or format, as long as you give appropriate credit to the original author(s) and the source, provide a link to the Creative Commons license and indicate if changes were made.

The images or other third party material in this chapter are included in the chapter's Creative Commons license, unless indicated otherwise in a credit line to the material. If material is not included in the chapter's Creative Commons license and your intended use is not permitted by statutory regulation or exceeds the permitted use, you will need to obtain permission directly from the copyright holder.

Chapter 8
Airbus Global Workforce Forecast (GWF)

Meet the Future Competence Challenge

Béatrice Pons, Jean-Hugues Rodriguez, and Florence Reuzeau

Abstract This chapter is a brief overview of the Global Workforce Forecast (GWF), a document made public by Airbus presenting the results of a large study launched by the group in 2018. The aim of the GWF is to provide every employee, every reader with relevant information and data to be prepared for the 2019–2029 competence challenge the company will face by 2030.

Keywords Human resources · Competencies · Industry 4.0 · Demography · Megatrends

8.1 Introduction

Understanding fast transitions (digitalisation, Industry 4.0, carbon neutral, COVID-19) and their transformations to come in different disciplines is key to be prepared for competence challenges. Our competence strategy resulting from successive iterations helps to anticipate declining activities, emerging jobs and competences.

The Global Workforce Forecast (GWF) document examines the main asset of the company, its human capital. It presents how to secure continuous positive growth and support Airbus' transition towards a new worldwide Industry 4.0 and becoming a new technology company. This document is structured into five main chapters: megatrends, demography, competence strategy, resource development levers and practices and the evolution of resource development levers.

B. Pons (✉) · J.-H. Rodriguez · F. Reuzeau
Airbus, Toulouse, France
e-mail: beatrice.pons@airbus.com

© The Author(s) 2022
H. Laroche et al. (eds.), *Managing Future Challenges for Safety*,
SpringerBriefs in Safety Management,
https://doi.org/10.1007/978-3-031-07805-7_8

8.2 Involve Everyone in the Transformation of the Company

It then appears obvious that each individual would need to take part in this transition by taking one's development into one's own hands with the support of the organisations. One way to facilitate this was the creation of a document providing all elements allowing "my" capability to project "myself" in future of "my" company in terms of skills.

The ambition of the Global Workforce Forecast is to provide all employees with relevant data, information and analysis to better understand, anticipate and prepare the evolution of our company competencies. Employees worldwide are actors of this opportunity and are encouraged to engage their own relevant development actions such as learning, mobility and knowledge management.

The purpose of this study launched in 2018 is to give a robust and consistent frame of reference to every reader in order to:

- access relevant data, information and analysis in a synthetic format;
- get a better understanding on current and future workforce evolution;
- get a better understanding of the current and future HR[1] levers supporting competence development from the organisation, team and employees;
- enable everyone to integrate these elements into their own decision-making process.

8.3 Deep and Fast Transformation: A Shared Concern

In 2019, Airbus decided to make this document public as all information provided could help institutions, universities, any talent worldwide and our supply chain employees and leaders to better understand our transitions and associated skills forecast. It was also considered as an opportunity to engage in exchanges with other stakeholders working on the subject, such as the World Economic Forum Future of Work, the EU Commission's Pact for Skills and other committees.

Our world is facing an ever-increasing pace of global change and has been labelled as volatile, uncertain, complex and ambiguous (VUCA). This world brings a high number of challenges and opportunities to our company: a competitive environment in a globalised and financially driven economy, a permanent increase in customer expectations, reputational challenges, the need for Airbus to deal with innovation mostly because of the COVID-19 crisis, the need to become carbon neutral, the digital transformation and the development of Industry 4.0, generational gaps and demographical changes considering that 50,000 employees will leave the company in the next 10 years and 80% of our staff will be generations Y, Z in 2027.

---

[1] Human Resource.

These fast-approaching transformations are conveying risks and challenges, but bring great opportunities if well anticipated and prepared with the full engagement of the whole organisation and all employees.

It is our company's responsibility to put in place appropriate means and levers helping managers and employees to adapt our main asset, "human capital", and make the most of it for a successful future with a positive growth mind-set.

Megatrends are transformative, global forces that shape the future world with their far-reaching influences on business, societies, economies, cultures and personal lives. Megatrends impact all regions of the world and all actors and organisations over a large time scale. We have selected six megatrends: economic globalisation, resource scarcity and climate change, global governance, demographics and social evolution, innovation and technologies, new consumption patterns.

8.4 The Airbus Competence Strategy: A Full Engagement with International Organisations

The Airbus competence strategy is a company approach which aims to support the business strategy implementation in a five year time frame and to accompany the five Airbus business drivers: boost our existing core business, be a digital aerospace champion, be a responsible company, be the global company of choice, shape the future of flight.

Consequently, the competence strategy objectives are to:

- assess external and internal evolutions and their impacts on jobs and competences;
- set up recommendations and actions to accompany these jobs and competence evolutions and reshaping;
- deploy all resource and develop actions to be taken by HR, academies, managers, employees to systematically serve our future needs;
- provide visibility to all employees on the competencies needed in the coming years for our business.

The Global Workforce Forecast helps also to understand the different HR tools and levers available to support skills development and knowledge sharing. A chapter is also dedicated to the improvement of those tools and levers. Leaders and employees should be more comfortable in engaging their collective and individual skills developments.

Analysis, realisation and communication of the Global Workforce Forecast open the door to different initiatives and communities worldwide:

- the World Economic Forum analysis and events for their "Future of Work";
- the European Commission's reflections on the subject and The Pact for Skills initiative on different ecosystems and particularly Aerospace and Defense;
- some national and regional working groups.

8.5 Conclusion

There is a clear ambition and willingness from many top leaders and specialists to find collective solutions in support of massive and scalable upskilling and reskilling challenges to respond to the impending fast transitions worldwide. The new technologies and the improved understanding of neuroscience open the door to very innovative approaches allowing new perspectives for easier responses to this challenge. Communication and open collaboration are key to engaging proper transitions with all stakeholders in education, industry (large and small companies), authorities, social partners and people.

Open Access This chapter is licensed under the terms of the Creative Commons Attribution 4.0 International License (http://creativecommons.org/licenses/by/4.0/), which permits use, sharing, adaptation, distribution and reproduction in any medium or format, as long as you give appropriate credit to the original author(s) and the source, provide a link to the Creative Commons license and indicate if changes were made.

The images or other third party material in this chapter are included in the chapter's Creative Commons license, unless indicated otherwise in a credit line to the material. If material is not included in the chapter's Creative Commons license and your intended use is not permitted by statutory regulation or exceeds the permitted use, you will need to obtain permission directly from the copyright holder.

Chapter 9
Rethinking Competencies in Hazardous Industries

Case Study of the Nuclear Sector in France

Alexandre Largier

Abstract Nuclear safety depends largely on the competence and competencies of the employees in the sector. While this is not a new subject, numerous current and future changes once again bring into question these competencies and their management. In recent years, a number of studies have demonstrated the limitations of the managerial approach to competencies, in particular their failure to take into account the collective dimension of said competencies and the contextual aspects of their implementation. In our opinion, competencies must be considered in terms of the work activity so that they are not restricted to a systematised formalism, and their management must be tackled within the organised framework in which they are deployed.

Keywords Competencies · Nuclear sector · Work activities

9.1 Introduction: Why Study Competencies in the Nuclear Industry?

French nuclear facilities are ageing, which raises new technical issues regarding the use or replacement of certain items of equipment, as well as the decommissioning work that can be expected. At the same time, the development of complex technologies—from digital twins to the use of artificial intelligence to identify probable failures, as well as the design of small modular reactors (SMRs)—reveals the critical importance of competence and competencies.

Meanwhile, the retirement of numerous workers in the nuclear sector in Europe and more especially in France, in addition to the poor opinion that younger generations have of the nuclear industry, raises questions regarding the development, and even the upkeep, of knowledge capital in the sector. This point is not new, as it was

---

A. Largier (✉)
IRSN, Fontenay-aux-Roses, France
e-mail: alexandre.largier@irsn.fr

© The Author(s) 2022
H. Laroche et al. (eds.), *Managing Future Challenges for Safety*,
SpringerBriefs in Safety Management,
https://doi.org/10.1007/978-3-031-07805-7_9

raised in the early 2000s by Mr. El Baradei,[1] Director General of the International Atomic Energy Agency (IAEA) from 1997 to 2009.

The way in which competencies in the nuclear industry are taken into account is related to the way in which people are integrated in socio-technical systems. This connection has evolved with the history of the sector and as a result of major nuclear accidents. It was after the accident at the Three Mile Island (TMI) power plant on 28 March 1979 that questions inherent to the training of operating staff came to be seen as being of major importance [11]. More recently, the accident at the Fukushima Daiichi power plant in Japan on 11 March 2011 can be considered as a new factor in the way competencies are taken into account in the nuclear industry. The earthquake and the tsunami that followed seriously affected the nuclear facilities as well as their environment. Consequently, providing support to the power plant agents proved complicated and, to a large extent, they had to cope on their own with a "beyond design" situation far exceeding the realm of what the plant was designed to withstand. Analysts at the time pointed out the importance of the resilience and competencies required to cope with unexpected events [12]. This accident raised questions, firstly, around the implementation of the competence and competencies of nuclear players in "extreme situations" [7] and, secondly, around the competencies of players not specifically belonging to the nuclear sector, but who are nevertheless stakeholders in crisis management (politicians, emergency services, medical staff, etc.).

Questions concerning the training and competencies of personnel working in the field of safety and radiation protection, therefore, fall within the scope of a long-term process marked by critical events. The subject of competence and competencies is not new, but has evolved further to these events and the questions they raised. They have led nuclear operators to define and deploy a set of systems to identify competency requirements in the short and medium terms, then evaluate, acquire and maintain said competencies.

However, this managerial approach to competencies has its limitations. In this document, we will attempt to describe them and to present an approach aimed at surpassing them.

9.2 Limitations of Managerial Approach to Competencies

In France, Strategic Workforce Planning (SWP) is built into the labour code: since 2005, all companies with more than 300 employees must renegotiate the SWP every three years. These companies, supported by management science researchers, have thus conducted long-term studies on the creation and deployment of a managerial approach to competencies.

While one undeniable advantage in taking these competencies into account has been the "production and renewal of numerous HRM (Human Resources Management) tools" [2, p. 40], the use of this concept has also led to studies on the work

---

[1] Speech by Mohamed El Baradei, during the IAEA general assembly in 2002.

itself and on workers (as opposed to qualifications focusing on workstations) and to more emphasis being placed on the role played by the work environment and its various components as contributing to the acquisition and mobilisation of such competencies. These two advantages—the development of a managerial approach to competencies and the work itself being taken into account—form the "competencies paradox". On the one hand, there is a move to standardise these competencies, and on the other hand, the assertion of a singularity that the systems struggle to encapsulate.

Most definitions of competency are based on elements put forward by ergonomics and psychology, where competence is defined as

> the individual taking initiative and responsibility for problems and events that they face in professional situations. […] a practical understanding of situations that relies on knowledge acquired and transforms them... [18, p. 70]

This transformation depends largely on resources that can be mobilised in a given situation and the abilities of the individual to mobilise them.

Presented in this way, competencies are transformed whenever they are implemented; they are what allows the player to take action in view of what is available and what is missing. It is, therefore, difficult to contain them in management systems that endeavour to normalise a situation in order to manage it. By attempting to specify and categorise competencies at all costs, we risk creating constraints that are too rigid or an administrative management that is disconnected from the reality of actual working situations, despite the fulfilment of such activities relying on the ability to adapt and invent new solutions.

Another limitation of the managerial approach to competencies lies in their individualising nature. While work requires increasingly collective activity to be performed, the managerial approach to competencies struggles to take into account the collective dimension of competencies.

This is evident in the way competence is evaluated, primarily on an individual basis [15], which is a major component of the "logic of competency" [14], at the core of the differentiation between players and their remuneration.

Despite these limitations, competence and competencies are always present as components of performance, both as regards production quality and industrial safety. Competencies are used in the texts of nuclear operators and regulators as an action lever and a guarantee of efficiency. Questions evolve, the subjects treated change, but competencies continue to be the centre of attention.

As an example, in 2004, the IRSN launched an analysis of the system managing the competencies of the operating personnel working for a nuclear operator. This study demonstrated that the competency reference frames, or "mandatory points of passage" of the competency approaches [13], are often highly detailed and consequently difficult to use. Similarly, the collective dimension of the activity is largely ignored by the management system, which also struggles to consider the competencies in a dynamic manner. Lastly, the deployment of the approach is incumbent upon the trades (mechanics, boilermaking, automation, etc.), while some activities, such as the monitoring of service providers, do not come under the role of a particular trade and find themselves partially "forgotten" by the management system [9].

The APTEIS[2] report entitled "Analyse de la chute du Générateur de Vapeur usé n°2 EDF—CNPE de Paluel" ("Analysis of the fall of the Paluel EDF—CNPE worn steam generator No. 2") published in 2017 confirms some of these results concerning competencies related to the monitoring activity, which corroborates the fact that the managerial approach to competencies has its limitations.

If the managerial approach to competencies has limitations, how can we tackle competencies whose implementation takes their singular nature into account, while also taking into consideration the needs of the companies, managers and operators who manage these competencies?

9.3 Rethinking Competencies in Work Activities

We do not consider that there are recommendations on the one side and actual work on the other, but rather that work is an activity that mobilises various resources—including recommendations—which must be understood, adapted and interpreted. The players' abilities to adapt are, therefore, not confined to a controlled area of freedom; they are inherent to the normality of work. According to Cuvelier and Woods [5], this "normal deviation" leads to the construction of competencies, instruments and work collectives. Competence is shaped by activities, by combining resources to reach the objective set in view of the specificities of the work situation. Competencies also establish the link between regulated safety and managed safety: effective safety is the expression of competencies implemented during the work activity, which mobilises various resources including recommendations. We, therefore, consider that competencies must be "taken seriously", in other words analysed firstly in their natural environment, that of the work "being done", and secondly considered with respect to the "organised framework" in which they lie and which they structure in return.

9.3.1 Analysing the Situational Implementation of Competencies

Competencies

> are not deployed in neutral universes, but in structured frameworks in which an employer expects the personnel or employees to comply with a hierarchical organisation, a division of the work, the scope of their "job" or "function", and to use the tools that have been imposed. [16, p. 89]

The resources (including know-how, tools, procedures and colleagues) are not always accessible, and the normative frameworks sometimes restrict the players, direct them,

---

[2] For "Analyse Pluridisciplinaire du Travail, Etudes et Interventions sociales", a group of experts specialising in multidisciplinary analysis of work and performing social studies.

even "prevent" them from being inventive. Knowledge is put into practice through relations—with managerial representatives, peers, customers—involving power relationships, effects of identity construction, belonging and self-image. The uses made of technical devices and systems that allow for competencies to be developed also contribute to players' strategies and behaviours. Competencies, therefore, consist of a dynamic combination insomuch as they are the result of mobilising knowledge and "supports" specific to the work context. They are remodelled each time the individuals and work collectives must "do what is necessary" to obtain an expected result, depending on their status at a given time and what is available. Consequently, the competencies implemented cannot be identified without analysing the situated activity.

9.3.2 Importance of Organisational Dimensions in the Implementation of Competencies

In order to act, individuals and collectives require internal and external resources and must be able to control the conditions necessary to access these resources. Yet, these resources are for the most part socially distributed and the product of the inscription of personal trajectories in interaction networks, organisations and institutional structures (labour market, etc.) [4, p. 15].

Thus, the contextualised implementation of resources depends partly on the individual path along which the individual acquires experience, develops certain competencies and loses others and weaves a network of potentially mobilisable interpersonal relations during the preparation and performance of the activity. Part of this path is determined by the organisation.

In theory, the development of the "logic of competency" in companies represents a shift away from seniority-based career development in which professional promotions are awarded purely for seniority at the expense of efficiency in the mobilisation of competencies and the level of performance reached. In reality, seniority-based and merit-based promotions coexist, which may cause some players to lose interest. In addition, increased professional mobility can only be exchanged for individual responsibility in the implementation and development of competencies if the internal job market available is sufficiently large. Otherwise, this may generate a feeling of imbalance, possibly even injustice, and lead the players to become demotivated [8]. Especially since today, there are numerous possibilities for developing a "side activity" [17], professional or not, simplified by communication and information technologies [3].

This possible disinvestment represents a double risk regarding safety and security. The first is that "jaded" players restrict themselves to "procedural compliance". Since industrial safety cannot be limited to a strict application of the rules, there is a strong chance that in this type of situation, the system will seize up. The second risk concerns the acquisition, development and maintenance of competencies. In trades where competencies are acquired in the long term, like most technical trades in the nuclear sector, the lack of perspectives and disinvestment could be prejudicial to the performance of the system.

Some authors consider that "enabling organisations", which promote the development of available resources and the possibilities of using them, must be designed [1, p. 113]. This approach illustrates the importance given to the context in which the competencies are implemented.

On the one hand, because the work context, near and far, serves as a support for the action. The resources present in the work environment—technical devices and systems, procedures, but also colleagues, customers, etc.—may be mobilised by the employees to reach their objectives. On the other hand, because the employees structure their work environment so that it offers "handholds" for the action.

9.4 Conclusion

Most of the activities performed include a collective dimension. They are the fruit of joint actions conducted within collectives where specific knowledge, routines, practices, standards and shared representations have been developed. This collective dimension of the activity, which is ignored by managerial approach of competencies, can be grasped through an analysis of the contextualised competencies, whereby the mobilisation of interpersonal networks and the periods of cooperation reveal the distributed and collective competencies [10].

Regarding safety, in the nuclear industry as in other sectors, to brush aside the aporias of a managerial approach to competencies too focused on single individuals and their know-how, we must analyse the work that goes into guaranteeing safety in a given context by mobilising and structuring the internal and external resources available and questioning the competencies related to this work (whether these competencies are focused on restructuring, finding workarounds, reorganisation or otherwise).

This situated approach towards competencies must also highlight the role of the "organised framework" on the implementation of competencies. The organisational measures set up to hire, train and foster progress for the players have an impact on the action itself, since they allow players to mobilise particular resources depending on procedures that are quite often specific to them. Conversely, players build this framework by creating rules, routines and systems; employees "fit out" their environment in such a way that it complies with and guides their action. This is made all the easier when the context is flexible.

Based on a situational analysis of the activity, a managerial approach to competencies should, therefore, firstly beware of any systematism and highlight the collective dimension of "safety work", including in the evaluation of the competencies and, secondly, consider how to make work environments more flexible. This approach would consist in adding value to surplus, asperities and duplicates, rather than erasing them.

Lastly, it may be worthwhile questioning the deployment of the "logic of competency" in organisations whose operation is still largely based on the planned organisation model [6]. Is there not a paradox, even an incompatibility, in implementing a logic advocating responsibility, autonomous and deliberate mobilisation in organisations where the activity is strictly defined and where players are expected to rigorously apply the rules and comply with the "best practices" enacted by the designers?

References

1. J. Arnoud, P. Falzon, Changement organisationnel et reconception de l'organisation: des ressources aux capabilités. Activités **10**(2), 109–130 (2013)
2. C. Batal, S. Fernagu-Oudet, Compétences, un folk concept en difficulté? Savoirs (3), 39–60 (2013)
3. T. Beauvisage, J. Beuscart, K. Mellet, Numérique et travail à-côté. Enquête exploratoire sur les travailleurs de l'économie collaborative. Sociologie du travail **60**(2) (2018)
4. J.-F. Bickel, V. Hugentobler, Les multiples faces du pouvoir d'agir à l'épreuve du vieillissement. Gérontologie et société **40**(157), 11–23 (2018)
5. L. Cuvelier, D. Woods, Sécurité réglée et/ou sécurité gérée : quand l'ingénierie de la résilience réinterroge l'ergonomie de l'activité. Le Travail Humain **82**(1), 41–66 (2019)
6. N. Dodier, Remarques sur la conscience du collectif dans les réseaux sociotechniques. Sociologie du travail **39**(2), 131–148 (1997)
7. F. Guarnieri, S. Travadel, C. Martin, A. Portelli, A. Afrouss, *L'accident de Fukushima Dai Ichi* (Presses des MINES, Paris, 2015)
8. N. Hatzfeld, L'individualisation des carrières à l'épreuve. Les grippages de la mobilité sur les chaines de Peugeot Sochaux. Soc. Contemp. **2**(54), 15–33 (2004)
9. A. Largier, Dispositif de gestion des compétences et logique métier. Socio-logos (3) (2008). Retrieved from https://journals.openedition.org/socio-logos/1323
10. A. Largier, C. Delgoulet, C. de la Garza, Quelle prise en compte des compétences collectives et distribuées dans la gestion des compétences professionnelles? Perspectives interdisciplinaires sur le travail et la santé **10**(1) (2008)
11. M. Llory, *L'accident de la centrale nucléaire de Three Mile Island: vingt ans après, nouvelles perspectives pour la sécurité, nouvelles inquiétudes* (L'Harmattan, Paris, 1999)
12. J.-C. Niel, L'après-Fukushima: la résilience des centrales nucléaires doit être renforcée. Annales des Mines, Responsabilité & Environnement **4**(72), 27–31 (2013)
13. E. Oiry, E. Sulzer, Les référentiels de compétences: enjeux et formes, in *La gestion des compétences. Acteurs et pratiques*, ed. by D. Brochier (Économica, Paris, 2002), pp. 29–47
14. C. Paradeise, Y. Lichtenberger, Compétences, compétence. Sociol. du Trav. **43**(1), 33–48 (2001)
15. F. Piotet, Compétence et ordre social, in *Réfléchir la compétence*, ed. by A. Dupray, C. Guitton, S. Monchatre (Octarès, Toulouse, 2003)
16. P. Ughetto, *Les nouvelles sociologies du travail. Introduction à la sociologie de l'activité* (De Boeck, Louvain-la-Neuve, 2018)
17. F. Weber, *Le travail à-côté* (Éditions de l'EHESS, Paris, 2009)
18. P. Zarifian, *Objectif compétences* (Éditions Liaisons, Paris, 1999)

Open Access This chapter is licensed under the terms of the Creative Commons Attribution 4.0 International License (http://creativecommons.org/licenses/by/4.0/), which permits use, sharing, adaptation, distribution and reproduction in any medium or format, as long as you give appropriate credit to the original author(s) and the source, provide a link to the Creative Commons license and indicate if changes were made.

The images or other third party material in this chapter are included in the chapter's Creative Commons license, unless indicated otherwise in a credit line to the material. If material is not included in the chapter's Creative Commons license and your intended use is not permitted by statutory regulation or exceeds the permitted use, you will need to obtain permission directly from the copyright holder.

Chapter 10
The Design of "Future Work" in Industrial Contexts

Lessons Learned from Worker–Technology Cooperation and Work Transformation Management

Flore Barcellini

Abstract This chapter proposes to discuss work transformation management as a key issue to designing working conditions to ensure safe, healthy and performant work in a context of technological transitions. Here, we view the design of future work as a transition process and as a set of projects—social, organisational, technological—that will together shape a "future of work". We consider lessons from the past regarding: (1) cooperation between workers and technology and (2) project management of work transformations, as resources to manage this transition. These lessons will be discussed with reference to ongoing research dealing with introduction of artificial intelligence (AI) or collaborative robotics at work in the French industrial context, as an illustration of the transformation of industry at a global level.

Keywords Worker–technologies cooperation · Transformation of work management · Activity-centred design · Ergonomics · Industry 4.0

10.1 Introduction

Work situations in industry are facing a profound transformation in relation to the introduction of technology due to both an evolution of this technology (evolutions of AI algorithms and massive data analysis, collaborative robotics…) and a political invitation at an international level [11] to promote the "modernisation" of industry. Indeed, a closer look at issues raised by technological transformations reveals that some "old" ones seem to be ignored by promotors of those transformations.[1] In this context, the objective of this chapter is to recall lessons learned concerning both workers-technology cooperation and work transformation management. We discuss

---

[1] See for instance [22] for an argumentation.

F. Barcellini (✉)
CNAM, Paris, France
e-mail: flore.barcellini@lecnam.net

the relevance of these lessons learned on the basis of several ongoing collaborative research projects dealing with introduction of collaborative robotics in industry line [5, 12, 30, 37] or artificial intelligence in various work situations (radiology, online counselling, legal activities, design and engineering) [5, 22, 23].[2]

In this chapter, we propose to discuss work transformation management as a key issue to designing "a future work" to ensure safe, healthy and performant work in a context of technological transitions. Here, we view the design of future work as a transition process and as a set of projects—social, organisational, technological—that will together shape a "future work" in a given situation. We focus here on lessons learned from the past regarding two key issues for managing this transition: (1) cooperation between workers and technology and (2) project management of work transformation, i.e. design project management.

10.2 Lessons Learned for Worker–Technology Cooperation Research and Project Design Management

10.2.1 Is Worker–Technology Cooperation a Myth or a Possible Reality?

Worker–technology cooperation has been studied at least since massive introduction of automation at work, as well as the first surge of artificial intelligence or expert systems in the late 80s, and in particular in relation to safety. Previous works on automation, AI and cooperation between human and machine sought to qualify the feasibility of human–machine cooperation and the risks implied for human health and organisational safety [26, 27, 35, 42]. These earlier works outlined limits such as impossibilities for an "intelligent or cooperative machine" to access and interpret context of action or to build a shared understanding of a worker situation, a poor relation between workers and technology that may be unidirectional and non-adaptative, i.e. the "machine" is not able to display dynamic behaviour in the course of the joint action with workers. These limits implied that the "machine" was not actually cooperative in a strong sense, as cooperation is anchored in the capacity of sharing common goals and of regulation of interdependent situations on the basis of understanding of a given situation of action [27, 39]. Technologies and workers were, thus, mainly in interdependence more than in cooperation [18, 26, 39, 42]. Regarding safety issues, these limits in the worker–technology relationship may imply [26]: loss of human expertise and lack of mutual control over a given situation, limited situation awareness construction and thus reliability of the worker–technology systems; complacency of workers regarding technology proposals and lack of self-confidence;

---

[2] ANR project HECTTOR ANR-17-CE10-0011; ANR project ICARO ANR-10-CORD-0025 on collaborative robotics. Collaboration with Orange Labs or car manufacturer on introduction of AI in various work situations (radiology, online counselling, legal activities, design and engineering).

and finally a lack of adaptivity of the worker–technology system due to a lack of anticipation and feedback [36]. Moreover, these limits are reviewed as being one cause of accidents [21, 38]. They can be explained by: (1) the limitations of the technology, the lack of in-depth modelling of human socio-cognitive activities [2, 16, 35]; but also (2) by the way, the introduction of technology is managed in particular with relation to socio-organisational consequences of technological changes, as outlined by the participatory approach and activity-centred ergonomics approach since the 70s [24, 40].

10.2.2 A Lack of a Participative and Work-Centred Project Management Approach in Introducing Cooperative Technology at Work

Indeed, several studies reveal that a majority of projects to introduce new technologies "fail" (60–80% according to studies [15]) with regards to delays in actual usage of new systems, budget overrun, goal achievement, safety and health issues [41]. Different models may be considered to explain these failures. There is extensive literature about a so-called resistance to change in organisations or an organisational inertia [20], the necessity of a cultural change or the role of leaders and managers [3]. However, there are several strong empirical and theoretical limitations to these models addressed by alternative research in ergonomics, sociology, organisation and management sciences (see [1, 7, 10, 24, 31, 33] for critics of previous models) revealing alternative causes of project failure: (1) the lack of political management and of actual cooperation in project management (weakness in the political management of the project and in the definition of project goals; poor collaboration of leaders; technically driven projects; absence of true participatory design approaches) and (2) the work that takes place in the organisations is approached only as a set of theoretical tasks in project management. The social and organisational dimensions of work are overlooked at the beginning of the projects and addressed only at a later stage, as consequences of technological choices. The constraints and leeway related to work activity, the consequences on health and on the quality of production or safety are poorly addressed. These may lead to some hazardous consequences for performance and health of workers, including safety and reliability. In order to overcome these pitfalls, some participative and work-centred project management approaches have been proposed for more than 40 years by participatory design or activity-centred ergonomics [24, 40]—sometimes supported by legislation successfully framing industrial relations as in Scandinavia [29], or not as the failed "Auroux" laws in France in the early 80s [28], and with more or rather less actual adoption in organisations.

10.3 So, Are Ongoing Transformations of Work in Relation to Technology Neglecting Lessons Learned from the Past?

As said in the introduction, industrial work situations are experiencing ongoing transformations in relation to introduction of technology (big data, RFID, virtual reality, AI, collaborative robotics…), these transformations are being encouraged by various national political programmes [11], such as "Industry 4.0" in Germany, "Industrie du futur" in France, "National Network for Manufacturing Innovation" in USA, "Manufacturing Industry Innovation 3.0 Strategy" in the UK, Made in China 2025. Here, the statement is that the globalisation of the financial market, coupled with the ageing of the working population and industrial facilities and ecological issues, may make it necessary to improve production plant and competitiveness. Moreover, the COVID-19 crisis may increase the wish to preserve and to develop a strong and innovative national industrial activity. So, what can be said about this "new era" of workers-technologies cooperation and the way introduction of these technologies is managed with regards to lessons learned from past research? To address these questions, we focus on two flagship "modernisation" technologies: AI and collaborative robotics, and we analyse proposals made by the French programme "Industrie du futur" to organise transformations, as it is claimed that this is one of the only national programmes which puts "Humans at the heart" of transformation.

10.3.1 A Strong Techno-Determinism, a Lack of Explainability and an Under-Estimation of the Socio-organisational Impacts of Technologies

Ongoing studies [5, 12, 22, 23] and analysis of the French "Industrie du Futur" programme using concepts and framework developed by activity-centred ergonomics and sociology [5, 30, 37] reveal a strong techno-determinism in the way technologies are still being conceived/thought of. Technologies are still seen as "remedies" to "problems" (e.g. competitiveness; safety…) with a lack of systematic analysis of those "problems". In addition, the possible consequences on company performance and worker health of the introduction of heterogeneous technologies "there and everywhere", without imagining their joint integration and the contradictions in everyday work that they may generate for workers, are not always considered. It is, however, necessary to assume there is a duality of "cooperation between workers and technology vs. subordination of workers to technology" and evaluate its risks for health, performance and safety, considering organisational and collective issues associated with the introduction of technologies. One can argue that some "old issues" are re-emerging nowadays even if they may be renewed by the enhanced performance of a "machine" [22, 37].

Concerning AI, Gamkrelidze et al. [22] pointed out that issues are tackled from an economical and technical angle, mainly to promote new AI systems. The same is observed for collaborative robotics[3] [34, 37]. Promotors of those technologies advocate for an *augmented* or *collaborative* approach between workers and technologies and not a *substitutive* approach. Beyond those promises, we observed in three studies [4, 12, 23] that collaborative robotics or AI still raise the question of actual cooperation between workers and technologies as well as questions about transformations of professional gestures, division of labour between workers and technologies, autonomy and responsibility of workers dependent of a machine behaviours, organisational issues or more societal job issues.

For instance, actual cooperative AI or systems should be able to understand the goals and actions of workers, and workers must be able to understand the functioning and decisions of AI or cooperative systems. This goal has not been reached yet as AI is still not really "explainable" [23]. In the same direction, collaborative robotics exemplified the promises—and pitfalls—of articulation between so-called cooperative technologies and evolution of work situations. On the "promises" side, this technology is presented as "easy to implement and to maintain"; "favouring productivity gains"; virtuous by making certain workstations more attractive for young workers or by contributing to the prevention of musculoskeletal disorders (MSD)—cobots taking over repetitive or strenuous tasks. This illustrates well the "technologies seen as remedies" perspective referred to above. On a previous project,[4] we tried to articulate technical and work-related issues in the design of a collaborative robot demonstrator intended to equip automobile assembly lines in order to prevent musculoskeletal disorders [5]. Although the demonstrator was not industrialised,[5] its design helped to understand technological locks related to dynamic regulation of interdependence between workers and cobots (e.g. dynamic re-planification of robot trajectories related to its analysis of the worker's position in space, gestures or direct communication). However, it was impossible to evaluate its potential role in MSD prevention. Indeed, the demonstrator was designed to reduce some of the biomechanical constraints incurred by workers, but it was only a necessary condition to prevent MSD and not a sufficient one. Indeed, design of the technology alone will not solve prevention and health issues; psychosocial dimensions of work, work organisation, interdependence between introduction of technology projects and other organisational projects related to the work situation [30] are as just as necessary—or even more so—than design of technological artefacts. Yet, in the former project, neither the evolution of the professional gestures nor collective or organisational issues related to the future work organisation were addressed. This advocates for strong proposals of work transformation project management approaches, in order to jointly design technologies and future work situations, including social and organisational issues.

---

[3] There is no consensus on the definition of cobot [32]. We will consider that cobots are robots assisting workers but remaining dependent on worker objectives and gestures. Cobots are thus seen as partners of workers with a direct physical interaction between them.

[4] ANR funded project ICARO ANR-10-CORD-0025.

[5] Because the demonstrator was too slow to cope with the pace of the industrial line.

10.3.2 A Claim for More Participative and Collaborative Project Management with a Lack of Operational Proposals

As said previously, there is a claim for the centrality of humans and a "vital" need to renew design and change management, but we outlined that those discourses are still dominated by technical rationality and political communication with a poor representation of human and labour sciences (ergonomics, occupational psychology, sociology of work, management and organisational sciences, adult education). Indeed, there is a lack of understanding and proposals regarding transformation of work situations and introduction of collaborative organisations. This is obvious, for example, in the "Industrie du Futur" programme and in the operational means that are proposed to companies to achieve their transformation. On the contrary, we observe a promotion of the Lean Management model as "the" model for so-called operational excellence [19] even though the limits of this model have been outlined in the French context [9]. Moreover, despite the wish for more "collaborative innovation" processes in industries, only technical or financial tools are proposed to help industries in coping with transformations and not really alternative project management approaches supporting actual collaboration of workers in designing their future work and developing the potentially relevant uses and usefulness of technologies as one of the resources of work [13]. Finally, the place left to "Humans" is reduced to training, with training programmes that mainly ignore the importance of "past" experience and the presumed outdated competences of workers to ensure performance and safety at work while assuming that training may compensate for a lack of anticipation of organisational evolutions of work situation questions regarding organisational issues. If humans and work are taken into account, it is often with an individual perspective and situated only at the workstation level, thus neglecting the collective dimension of work and its role in—once again—preserving performance, safety and health.

10.4 What Recommendations to Foster the Success of Projects in Terms of Health, Safety and Performance?

Here, we advocate for widespread promotion and experience of participatory or activity-centred ergonomics project design management approaches [6, 8, 17, 24] as good candidates for one of the "collaborative innovation" approaches. These approaches are designed to address political, social, organisational and technical issues related to work transformation. Indeed, the finality in work transformation related to introduction of technologies has less to do with the characteristics of the technologies themselves (products, tools, working spaces, workstations, organisation, technologies, etc.) as with the *work situations*—articulating individual, social, organisational and technological dimensions—in which these technologies are present. It assumes that work transformation projects are decision-making and design processes [14], socially determining work situations (i.e. structured by a set of decisions made by CEO, designers or prescribers of work in general) and defining a set of prescriptions (tasks to be carried out, technologies to work with organisational structure staff allocation, contracts, timetables, rules, etc.) that workers will have to cope with [25]. In order to be successful, these approaches argue that: (1) an effective political management of work transformation articulating and organising debates and negotiation within the different logics at stake in the project (technology, safety, health, production, human resources, etc.) in a systemic way is needed; (2) and that the decision-making process must be grounded in an understanding and a modelling of actual and future work situations based on an in situ activities analysis.

Acknowledgements This chapter is based on past and current collaborations during the ANR ICARO (Corinne Grosse, Adolfo Suarez, Antoine Lasnier, Nahid Armande, colleagues from LAAS and Lirmm) and HECTTOR (Caroline Moricot, Anne-Cécile Lafeuillade, Willy Buchmann, Tahar-Hakim Benchekroun, Marco Saraceno, Celine Rosselin, Thierry Pillon, Gérard Dubey, Ali Siadat, Mouad Bounouar, Richard Béarée) projects and a collaboration with Orange Labs (Moustafa Zouinar, Tamari Gamkrelidze).

References

1. M. Akrich, Beyond social construction of technology: the shaping of people and things in the innovation process, in *New Technology at the Outset*, ed. by M. Dierkes, U. Hoffmann (Campus/Westview, Frankfurt/New-York, 1992), pp. 173–190
2. R. Amalberti, *La conduite des systèmes à risque* (PUF, collection "Le travail humain", Paris, 2001)
3. D. Autissier, I. Vandangeon-Derumez, Pas de changement sans adhésion des managers. L'Expansion Manag. Rev. **126**(3), 116–129 (2007)
4. F. Barcellini, Industry of the future: which place for work and its transformation? in *Moving Work*, ed. by M.L. Emilie Bourdu (Presses des Mines, 2019)
5. F. Barcellini, Conception of human-robot collaborative cooperation. A case of participation in a collaborative robot design process. Activités **17**(1) (2020)
6. F. Barcellini, L. Van Belleghem, F. Daniellou, Design projects as opportunities for the development of activites, in *Constructive Ergonomics*, ed. by P. Falzon (Taylor & Francis, New York, USA, 2014), pp. 187–204
7. E. Beck, P for political: participation is not enough. Scand. J. Inf. Syst. **14**(1) (2002)
8. P. Béguin, Design as a mutual learning process between user and designers. Interact. Comput. **15**(5), 709–730 (2003)
9. T.-H. Benchekroun, J. Arnoud, R. Arama, Vitalité des activités et rationalité du Lean: deux études de cas. Perspectives interdisciplinaires sur le travail et la santé (2013). https://doi.org/10.4000/pistes.3589
10. P. Bernoux, *Sociologie du changement dans les entreprises et les organisations* (Seuil, Paris, 2004)
11. T. Bidet-Mayer, *L'industrie du futur : une compétition mondiale* (Presses des Mines, Paris, 2016)
12. M. Bounouar, R. Béarée, A. Siadat et al., On the role of human operators in the design process of cobotic systems. Cogn. Tech. Work. **24**, 57–73 (2022). https://doi.org/10.1007/s10111-021-00691-y

13. G. Bourmaud, P. Rabardel, From computer to instrument system: a developmental perspective. Interact. Comput. **15**(5), 665–691 (2003)
14. L. Bucciarelli, An ethnographic perspective on engineering design. Des. Stud. **9**, 159–168 (1988)
15. M. Combes, L. Lethielleux, Comment prédire et expliquer l'échec des changements organisationnels. Rev. Fr. Gest. **188–189**(8), 325–339 (2008)
16. F. Daniellou, *L'opérateur, la vanne, l'écran: l'ergonomie des salles de contrôles* (Editions de l'ANACT, 1986)
17. F. Daniellou, P. Rabardel, Activity-oriented approaches to ergonomics: some traditions and communities. Theor. Issues Ergon. Sci. **5**, 353–357 (2005)
18. S.W. Dekker, D.D. Woods, MABA-MABA or abracadabra? Progress on human-automation co-ordination. Cogn. Technol. Work **4**(4), 240–244 (2002)
19. FIM, *Guide pratique de l'usine du futur: enjeux et panorama de solutions* (Fédération des Industries Mécaniques, 2016). Retrieved from http://industriedufutur.fim.net/wp-content/uploads/2015/11/Guide_pratique_UDF.pdf
20. J. Ford, L. Ford, A. d'Amelio, Resistance to change: the rest of the story. Acad. Manag. Rev. **33**(2), 362–377 (2008)
21. K. Funk, B. Lyall, J. Wilson, R. Vint, M. Niemczyk, C. Suroteguh, G. Owen, Flight deck automation issues. Int. J. Aviat. Psychol. **9**, 109–123 (1999)
22. T. Gamkrelidze, M. Zouinar, F. Barcellini, The "old" issues of the "new" artificial intelligence systems in professional activities, in *Digital Transformation in the Challenge of Activity and Work*, ed. by M. Bobillier-Chaumon (ISTE Wiley, London, UK, 2021), pp. 71–86
23. T. Gamkrelidze, M. Zouinar, F. Barcellini, Working with machine learning/artificial intelligence systems: workers' viewpoints and experiences, in *ECCE 2021: European Conference on Cognitive Ergonomics 2021*, Article 14 (2021)
24. A. Garrigou, F. Daniellou, G. Carballeda, S. Ruaud, Activity analysis in participatory design and analysis of participatory design activity. Int. J. Ind. Ergon. **15**, 311–327 (1995)
25. F. Guerin, A. Laville, J. Durrafourg, F. Daniellou, A. Kerguelen, *Understanding and Transforming Work: The Practices of Ergonomics* (ANACT Network Editions, Lyon, France, 2006)
26. J. Hoc, Towards a cognitive approach to human-machine cooperation in dynamic situations. Int. J. Human-Comput. Stud. **54**, 509–540 (2001). https://doi.org/10.1006/ijhc.2000.0454
27. J. Hoc, P. Cacciabue, E. Hollnagel, *Expertise and Technology: Cognition and Human-Computer Cooperation* (Lawrence Erlbaum, New Jersey, USA, 1995)
28. C. Howell, The contradictions of French industrial relations reform. Comp. Polit. **24**(2), 181–197 (1992)
29. A. Kanstrup, D for democracy: on political ideals. Participatory Des. Scand. J. Inf. Syst. **15**(1) (2003)
30. A. Lafeuillade, F. Barcellini, W. Buchmann, T. Benchekroun, Integrating collaborative robotics into work situations: the intentions of SME managers in the digital transformations of their companies, in *Digital Transformation in the Challenge of Activity and Work*, ed. by M. Bobillier-Chaumon (ISTE Wiley, London, UK, 2021), pp. 115–128
31. S. Lapeyrière, Les aventures de Substance et Cohérence au pays des projets. Le Travail Humain **50**(2), 125–132 (1987)
32. T. Moulières-Seban, *Conception de systèmes cobotiques industriels: approche cognitive : application à la production pyrotechnique au sein d'Ariane Group*. Ph.D. thesis, Université de Bordeaux, 2017. Retrieved from https://tel.archives-ouvertes.fr/tel-01697610
33. A. Nascimento, Organizational change, cultural change? Insights for ergonomic intervention. Le travail humain **83**(2), 161–177 (2020)
34. M. Peshkin, J.E. Colgate, Cobots. Ind. Robot. **26**(5), 335–341 (1999)
35. P. Rabardel, *Human and Technologies: Cognitive Approaches of Contemporary Instruments* (Armand Colin, 1995)
36. J. Reason, Cognitive aids in process environments: prostheses or tools?, in *Cognitive Engineering in Complex Dynamic Worlds*, ed. by E. Hollnagel, G.G. Mancini, D. Woods (Academic Press, London, 1988), pp. 7–14

37. M. Saraceno, (2020) L'homme «au cœur». Du robot au cobot, le mythe du «bon» automate dans la médiatisation de «l'industrie du futur» (1978–2018). Communications **37**(1)
38. N. Sarter, D.D. Woods, "How in the world did we get into that mode?" Mode error and awareness in supervisory control. Hum. Factors **37**, 5–19 (1995)
39. K. Schmidt, Remarks on the complexity of cooperative work. Revue d'Intelligence Artificielle **16**(4–5), 443–483 (2002)
40. J. Simonsen, T. Robertson, *Routledge International Handbook of Participatory Design* (Routledge, NY, USA, 2012)
41. A. Wisner, F. Daniellou, Operation rate of robotized systems: the contribution of ergonomic work analysis, in *Human Factors in Organizational Design and Management*, ed. by H. Hendrick, O. Brown (Elsevier Science Publishers B.V, Amsterdam, The Netherlands, 1984), pp. 461–465
42. M. Zouinar, Évolutions de l'Intelligence Artificielle: quels enjeux pour l'activité humaine et la relation Humain Machine au travail? Activités **17**(1) (2020). Retrieved from https://doi.org/10.4000/activites.4941

Open Access This chapter is licensed under the terms of the Creative Commons Attribution 4.0 International License (http://creativecommons.org/licenses/by/4.0/), which permits use, sharing, adaptation, distribution and reproduction in any medium or format, as long as you give appropriate credit to the original author(s) and the source, provide a link to the Creative Commons license and indicate if changes were made.

The images or other third party material in this chapter are included in the chapter's Creative Commons license, unless indicated otherwise in a credit line to the material. If material is not included in the chapter's Creative Commons license and your intended use is not permitted by statutory regulation or exceeds the permitted use, you will need to obtain permission directly from the copyright holder.

Chapter 11
Standardization and Risk Regulation for High-Hazard Industries

Michael Baram and Corinne Bieder

Abstract Hazardous industrial activities have historically been regulated from a safety and/or risk management viewpoint based on regulations enacted by governmental authorities. This chapter describes and explains the decline in the role played by governmental actors in the process of safety regulation and the rise of private standards development organizations. Such an evolution raises a wide range of concerns regarding the incentives to enhance safety, the interests that are protected by standards endorsed by regulators, and at a societal level, the drift away from democratic governance of high-hazard activities.

Keywords Standardization · Regulation · Governance · High-risk industries · Safety

11.1 Introduction

Government regulation has played a major role in shaping the safety management programs and practices of companies engaged in high-hazard activities. But, there are many other forces at work in modern society that also influence safety management such as negligence liability, insurance coverage, investor decisions, behavioral norms, and increasingly, the development of national and international standards by both private and public sector standards developing organizations (SDOs).

The scope and scale of private standardization activities are vast. Worldwide, thousands of private SDOs engage in setting a multitude of voluntary standards that become available for adoption by national regulators, companies, legislators, and international organizations [18]. In addition, governments are now using standardization to address the governance of new technologies. A survey of the comprehensive

M. Baram (✉)
School of Law, Boston University, Boston, MA, USA
e-mail: mbaram@bu.edu

C. Bieder
ENAC, University of Toulouse, Toulouse, France

© The Author(s) 2022
H. Laroche et al. (eds.), *Managing Future Challenges for Safety*,
SpringerBriefs in Safety Management,
https://doi.org/10.1007/978-3-031-07805-7_11

US Code of Federal Regulations reveals that US agencies have adopted over 10,000 privately developed standards and, by doing so, made them enforceable regulations.[1] In the EU, three official organizations are striving to harmonize standards adopted by 33 countries and are also directing the development of new EU standards for topics such as artificial intelligence (AI).[2]

This chapter focuses mainly on private standardization that is relevant to industrial safety. It begins with a discussion of the growing role that such standards play in shaping risk regulation and then considers factors that motivate and empower private SDOs, the benefits and challenges that SDOs pose to self-regulation, and the platforms that SDOs provide that enable industry-led governance of new technologies. Further discussion highlights concerns about growing societal reliance on privately developed standards, and the EU and US focus on the "trustworthiness" criterion for artificial intelligence standards, the subordination of safety regulation, and the drift away from democratic governance of high-hazard activities.

11.2 Interplay Between Standards and Risk Regulation

For decades, national and international standards for products, processes, engineering and management practices have been developed by SDOs for many purposes: e.g., overcome trade barriers, advance the safety of consumer products and industrial equipment, promote interoperability of multiple products, and gain competitive advantage [3]. Well-known examples are voluntary standards for home appliances, communication systems, medical equipment, construction materials, fire protection, food safety, pressure vessels, and many engineering systems and practices.

The largest private SDOs, the International Organization for Standardization (ISO) (over 23,000 standards)[3] and the Institute of Electrical and Electronic Engineers (IEEE) (over 1200 standards)[4], proclaim their neutrality and independence and enlist global networks of experts, governmental and company representatives for participation in their standard-setting proceedings. Among other types of SDOs are industrial and trade associations that develop consensus standards which reflect the economic, safety, and other interests of their member companies. For example, in the oil and gas sector, standards have been developed by SDOs such as the American Petroleum Institute (API) (over 700 standards)[5] and its Norwegian counterpart, Norsok (79 standards).[6]

---

[1] National Institute for Standards and Technology, Standards incorporated by reference database (showing 11,259 total incorporations by référence as of December 20, 2014): https://standards.gov/.

[2] https://www.cencenelec.eu/.

[3] https://www.iso.org/.

[4] https://www.ieee.org/.

[5] https://www.api.org/.

[6] https://www.standard.no/.

Most standards relevant to the safety of hazardous industrial activities apply to the design, testing, and performance of the products, systems, materials, and equipment involved. But, safety-relevant *management* standards have also been enacted. Some are generic and applicable to many different industrial sectors, such as ISO 9000 on Quality Management, ISO 45001 on Occupational Health and Safety, ISO 14000 on Environmental Management, and ISO 31000 on Risk Management. Other standards provide technical detail for the design and operation of industrial systems, such as IEEE standards on protection and coordination of industrial power systems, secure communication networks, and surveillance testing of nuclear safety systems. Finally, UN agencies and other international organizations enact voluntary standards to advance human rights, sustainability, resilience, transparency, and corporate social responsibility [12, 20], (OECD; World Bank). Obviously, companies that adopt any of these types of standards must adapt their safety management systems accordingly.

Many privately developed voluntary standards subsequently become enforcible regulations. Government policies (EU, US) tell regulators who intend to develop a new rule to instead consider adopting or incorporating by reference a relevant private voluntary standard and have it serve as their own regulation.[7,8] This enables regulators to capitalize on the expertise and industry support developed by SDOs, substantially reduce the regulator's costs and administrative burdens, and keep pace with rapid technological advances.

In the US, most regulation of industrial safety and prevention of major accidents is prescriptive and technically detailed. A regulator who intends to develop a new rule but avoids adopting a relevant private standard is likely to encounter opposition by the targeted industry and be caught up in lengthy adversarial proceedings. Thus, it is no surprise that US regulators have readily chosen the private standard option that embodies the expertise and industrial support developed by the SDO. As a result, in the oil and gas sector in the US and many other countries, virtually all regulations on exploration and production operations are prescriptive versions of hundreds of voluntary standards originally developed by API [2].

In the EU, the regulatory approach to industrial safety is more likely to be performance-based and self-regulatory in that companies are expected to determine how to fulfill safety management functions and perform operations safely. Although companies had sought this flexibility, once gained, many thereafter seek detailed guidance on how to comply with the broad mandate for self-regulation and call upon regulators to provide such guidance. In the Norwegian oil and gas sector, guidances and mentoring are provided by regulators with persuasive reference to relevant voluntary standards set by Norsok and other SDOs [13].

Thus, privately developed standards become essential features of both the self-regulatory and prescriptive approaches to industrial safety [14], and this interplay, as the oil and gas examples indicate, leads to societal dependence on private SDOs and

---

[7] European Commission, *Standardization Policy*, https://ec.europa.eu/info/.

[8] American National Standards Institute, U.S. Standards System: https://www.standardsportal.org/ (last accessed on 07/09/2021); and the National Technology Transfer and Advancement Act, 15 U.S.C 3701 et seq.

the subordination of safety regulation. Although a low-visibility feature of modern risk governance, this trend needs to be better understood and aligned with public policies and norms.

11.3 Toward a Better Understanding of Standardization

The universe of private SDOs can be seen as a global knowledge-producing infrastructure that serves the standardization needs of companies, countries, non-governmental organizations, trade groups, and many others [23]. It is subordinating and replacing government regulation, thereby bringing about a de facto change in public policy. It is, therefore, essential to gain a better understanding of the standardization infrastructure and its influence on regulation and management of industrial safety.

The public–private divide between most standardization and regulation needs to be kept in mind. Regulation (and its co-regulatory and self-regulatory variants) is a government-created framework for transparently making decisions in the public interest. Open to stakeholders and public involvement, regulation employs established procedures and follows substantive mandates that are aligned with societal norms and public policies, and it provides for accountability. In contrast, standardization is a fragmented, unregulated, opaque field populated mainly by privately owned and financed SDOs who set their own procedures, usually exclude public involvement, disregard transparency and restrict access to documentation, and make self-serving, private-interest decisions that are usually driven by economic considerations. Simply put, regulation is public domain, standardization is private domain (unless directed by government as in the case of the EU's single market program), and arranging for their complementarity is the main societal task at hand [5].

As discussed earlier, two types of standards are often safety-relevant. *Technical and engineering practice standards* number in the thousands, and usually apply to the design and performance of an extremely broad range of products, their design, interchangeability, interoperability, and their integration into systems, processes, and controls. *Management standards* are few but adopted by many and apply to structure, procedures, functions, tasks, communications, quality control, and other aspects of an organization's system for meeting its goals.

Regulators often adopt or incorporate by reference such standards as generically applicable rules or as highly persuasive (de facto mandatory) referential guidances as discussed earlier. This supports regulatory programs that are prescriptive and take a one-size fits-all approach to safety. But when done routinely to facilitate industrial compliance with a self-regulatory program, it can harden the program's soft law approach to industrial safety [18].

The initial claim of soft law/self-regulation was to provide some leeway for companies to consider their unique circumstances and accordingly define their own best-practice approach to safety management. But, the massive adoption of detailed technical standards leads back to a prescriptive approach to safety, where individuals and organizations at all levels are expected to follow referential standards and guidances for compliance. Thus, standardization can facilitate industrial compliance with self-regulation but can also transform self-regulation into a prescriptive regime.

Standardization of management systems can also work against another intended benefit of self-regulation, that self-regulation would enable a progression of advances in risk analysis and safety culture by experts in these fields. But, management standards such as those set by ISO incorporate knowledge from many fields which may be outdated, biased, or based on insufficient expertise, yet because of their widespread adoption, such standards may enable a "cementation of inadequate principles and methods" [1].

Among its other attributes, standardization provides platforms for industrial leadership on important societal issues that legislators and regulators have failed to fully address [21]. Private SDOs such as API can be expected to integrate and imbed industrial positions on environmental, societal, and governance (ESG) issues (e.g., sustainability, climate change, privacy) in their standards and thereby enable industry leadership on the issues before public awareness and discourse and before government positions are taken [15].

Finally, it is well-established that most privately developed standards are designed to serve the economic and private interests of their developers rather than deciding solely upon best practices for workplace and societal safety. This obviously raises questions regarding the relevance or value of having these standards serve as references to fulfill an organizations' self-regulatory responsibilities. Safety-relevant standards also incorporate assumptions as to the characteristics of high-risk organizations and their operational context, assumptions that correspond to the characteristics of the organizations involved in developing the standards. Although the assumptions may not be realistic or acceptable for many other organizations not part of the SDOs, the standards will serve as references in their cases as well.[9]

Despite these observations, standardization is of great value to the global economy and technological advancement, and as discussed earlier, there are pragmatic reasons for its proliferation and power. It shapes regulation and enables self-regulation, helps industry take the lead in societal governance of new technologies, and avoids the bureaucracy, procedures, public involvement, costs, and politics associated with regulation. It enlists expertise and industrial support rapidly and is more capable of keeping pace with technological advances. It is promoted by legislators and regulators. Its SDOs are unaccountable participants in risk governance. And it creates markets and technical and commercial collaborations, enables competitive advantage, gains safe harbor from negligence liability, and secures regulatory outcomes that fit the practices and interests of the entities involved. But even the most ardent proponents of standardization recognize the need to have this private enterprise complement safety regulation and align with public policies [21].

---

[9] An industrial SDO may lose member companies that have more progressive policies on corporate societal responsibilities. See Total Withdraws from the American Petroleum Institute (15/01/2021).

11.4 Standardization and AI

Perhaps the most important attributes of private standardization are its ability to generate the technical knowledge needed for soft law governance of new technologies and its enabling of relationships and transactions between developers of the technologies, users, investors, and governments. These relationships are essential for the financing, interoperability, implementation, and commercial success of the technologies [7].

The case of artificial intelligence (AI) is instructive. The EU and the US are committed to deriving societal value from AI but worry that governance too stringent will stifle its further development and applications and are, therefore, cautiously issuing interim policy statements and guidances that are leading to self-regulatory/soft law governance of AI [9, 17]. Foreseeable problems are being addressed, involving, for example, access to proprietary information, monopolistic practices, and allocation of liability for harms [8].

Both regimes are confronted by widespread public concerns about the value and societal impacts of AI itself and about potential misuse and unintended consequences when put to use in an unlimited range of applications. This has led both the EU and US to identify and define the core issue of the "trustworthiness" of AI and create interim *principles of trustworthiness* (often referred to as "ethical principles") for AI developers and users to self-assess the acceptability of their AI systems and applications. Trustworthiness principles common to both the EU and US include accuracy, explainability, reliability and resilience, privacy, safety, mitigation of bias, transparency, fairness, and accountability, with the EU list adding an emphasis on ensuring informed human involvement in decision-making and oversight [10, 11]; (NIST n.d.).

These broad principles for self-assessment provide the basis for an extremely loose and ineffective form of self-regulation unless further defined for use in actual cases, and credible oversight, mentoring, and accountability functions are established through government-industry co-regulation. A co-regulatory approach with these features is especially important for AI applications to workplace safety and safety management systems for the prevention of major accidents such as surveillance and remote control of operations and evaluation of near miss incidents.

Given the evidence that governments are reluctant to regulate AI, it can be expected that the EU and US approaches will be extremely reliant on private standardization of AI applications and the trustworthiness/ethical principles. A cascade of private standards is already underway with the IEEE announcing its finalization of 14 voluntary AI standards and associated compliance certification programs on topics ranging from algorithmic bias to well-being metrics for ethical AI. Not to be outdone, ISO has 31 voluntary AI-related standards ready for adoption or use as guidance, or in progress, including a forthcoming standard for AI risk management.

As a result, concerns about the proliferation of AI standards are being expressed such as the hardening of the self-regulatory or co-regulatory approach, the difficulty of assessing numerous standards to identify gaps and contradictions, and the need for a coordinating entity [16]. The path forward will be difficult unless responsible oversight and direction is brought about by private–public collaboration.

11.5 A Concerning Trend in Progress

The reliance of regulators on privately developed standards is not new. It had already become common practice since the emergence of self-regulation in the 1980s. Self-regulation was presented as a step change in the management of industrial safety, leaving more leeway to high-hazard companies to define the safety enhancement measures best suited to their characteristics and circumstances as opposed to routinely complying with generic standards prescribed by regulators. A close look at what led to more self-regulation and more standardization at that time shows that the fast pace of technological advances and the limited resources available to regulators were key elements outweighing ambitions to enhance safety [4].

The situation has not changed since then. Technology is still fast and requires fast response for its governance and the adaptation of safety management systems, whereas regulatory processes remain cumbersome and slow. Furthermore, regulators lack expertise to keep up to speed with new and evolving technologies and have budget limitations preventing them from recruiting the best experts or developing the required competences in-house. Privately developed standards circumnavigate some of these challenges and quickly provide pragmatic results. However, this growing public reliance on privately developed standards entails critical concerns.

Privately developed standards can be considered a missed chance to significantly improve safety in practice. Standards developed by industrial SDOs are meant to protect and advance the interests of their members. Setting very high-level standards inspired by the best practices of the most safety-mature member organizations would do no good for and, be opposed by, the least progressive members. Therefore, standards developed by private SDOs are instead aligned with the practices of the least progressive, providing no incentive or insights for organizations to do better safety-wise. This fall back on standards with limited ambition enables "business as usual" and also serves another purpose that is dear to the SDOs member companies. Adopting them is easy and helps to establish a "safe harbor" against negligence liability for these companies.

The universe of private SDOs is unregulated, and its uncoordinated response to a new technology such as AI with a multitude of standards can create difficulties in assessing and putting them to use. Reliance on such standards for effective self-regulation and highly valued interoperability outcomes requires responsible public–private leadership to carry out oversight, coordination, and harmonization functions.

At a broader societal level, the increasing role of privately developed standards in the governance framework leads to neglecting or crowding out public interest perspectives. Whereas regulators are meant to represent the voice of the society, the process of developing standards by private SDOs usually does not provide for transparency nor the involvement of stakeholders that represent a balancing of different societal interests and norms [6].[10] In that respect, reliance on private standards escapes the democratic process that regulators are supposed to follow and resembles the contractual outsourcing of governmental decision-making functions. In the absence of representation of other interests beyond that of industrial organizations, economic value becomes the main driver in standards development, and cost–benefit analysis becomes the main decision tool for deciding what a standard should provide.

The democratic deficit that is incurred by the privatization of regulation reaches beyond the opaqueness of standards development. Many standards involve proprietary information, and thus cannot be explained. Although standard-setters claim that ethical and other societal interests are incorporated in the standards, there is often no way to know the details of what was done exactly and how or to test the standards.

Thus, all these issues involved by the regulatory reliance on private standardization reflect a concerning drift away from democratic governance of hazardous industrial activities.

References

1. T. Aven, M. Ylonen, The strong power of standards in the safety and risk fields. Reliab. Eng. Syst. Saf. **189**, 279–286 (2019)
2. M. Baram, The US Regulatory regime for preventing major accidents in offshore operations, in *Risk Governance of Offshore Oil and Gas Operations*, ed. by P. Lindøe, M. Baram, O. Renn (Cambridge University Press, 2014), pp. 154–187
3. M. Baram, K. McAllister, Private voluntary self-regulation, in *Alternatives to Regulation*, ed. by M. Baram (Lexington Books, 1982), pp. 53–76
4. C. Bieder, Safety science: a situated science: an exploration through the lens of safety management systems. Saf. Sci. **135** (2021)
5. E. Bremer, Private complements to public governance. 81 Mo. Law Rev. pp. 1116–1125 (2016). Retrieved from https://scholarship.law.missouri.edu/mlr/vol81/iss4/14
6. J. Contreras, Understanding balance requirements for standards-development organizations. CPI Antitrust Chronicle (2) (2019). Retrieved from https://ssrn.com/abstract=3454894
7. DIN, *The Economic Benefits of Standardization* (ASTM Business Link, 2001). Retrieved from www.DIN.de
8. M. Ebers, Regulating explainable AI in the European Union: an overview of the current legal framework(s), in *Nordic Yearbook of Law and Informatics 2020: Law in the Era of Artificial Intelligence*, ed. by L. Colonna, S. Greenstein (2021). Retrieved from https://ssrn.com/abstract=3901732
9. European Commission, *White Paper on Artificial Intelligence-A European Approach to Excellence and Trust*. White paper, European Commission, COM, Brussels, 2020
10. European Commission Expert Group, *Ethics Guidelines for Trustworthy AI* (European Commission, 2019). Retrieved from op.europa.eu
11. Executive Office of the President, *Promoting the Use of Trustworthy Artificial Intelligence in the Federal Government*. Federal Register (EO 13960) (2020). Retrieved from https://www.federalregister.gov/documents/2020/12/08/2020-27065/promoting-the-use-of-trustworthy-artificial-intelligence-in-the-federal-government

---

[10] CEN-CENELEC, Standardization and Societal Stakeholders at cencenelec.eu (last accessed 07/09/2021).

12. I. Higham, UN guiding principles on business and human rights, in *Standardization and Risk Governance*, ed. by E. Olsen, K. Juhl, P.H. Lindøe, O. Engen (Routledge, 2020), pp. 217–234
13. K. Kaasen, Safety regulation on the Norwegian continental shelf, in *Risk Governance of Offshore Oil and Gas Operations*, ed. by P. Lindøe, M. Baram, O. Renn (Cambridge University Press, 2014), pp. 103–131
14. P. Lindøe, M. Baram, The role of standards in hard and soft approaches to safety regulation, in *Standardization and Risk Governance*, ed. by E. Olsen, K. Juhl, P. Lindøe, O. Engen (Routledge, 2020), pp. 235–254
15. J. Macey, Why is the ESG focus on private companies, not the government? Bloomberg Law (2021). Retrieved from https://news.bloomberglaw.com/esg/why-is-the-esg-focus-on-private-companies-not-the-government
16. G. Marchant, Soft law governance of artificial intelligence. *AI Pulse* (2019). Retrieved from https://aipulse.org/soft-law-governance-of-artificial-intelligence/
17. G. Marchant, L. Tournas, C. Gutierrez, Governing emerging technologies through soft law: lessons for artificial intelligence. Jurimetrics **61**(1) (2020)
18. W. Mattli, T. Buthe, Setting international standards: technological rationality or primacy of power? World Polit. **56**, 1–42 (2003)
19. NIST, *AI Risk Management Framework* (n.d.)
20. OECD, *Guidelines for Multinational Enterprises* (n.d.). Retrieved from OECD: www.oecd.org
21. WEF, *Agile Regulation for the Fourth Industrial Revolution: A Toolkit for Regulators* (World Economic Forum, 2020). Retrieved from http://www3.weforum.org
22. World Bank, *Environmental and Social Performance Standards for Private Sector Activities* (n.d.). Retrieved from World Bank. www.worldbank.org
23. J. Yates, C. Murphy, *Engineering Rules: Global Standard Setting Since 1880* (Johns Hopkins University Press, 2019)

Open Access This chapter is licensed under the terms of the Creative Commons Attribution 4.0 International License (http://creativecommons.org/licenses/by/4.0/), which permits use, sharing, adaptation, distribution and reproduction in any medium or format, as long as you give appropriate credit to the original author(s) and the source, provide a link to the Creative Commons license and indicate if changes were made.

The images or other third party material in this chapter are included in the chapter's Creative Commons license, unless indicated otherwise in a credit line to the material. If material is not included in the chapter's Creative Commons license and your intended use is not permitted by statutory regulation or exceeds the permitted use, you will need to obtain permission directly from the copyright holder.

Chapter 12
Adaptive Imagination at Work in Health Care

Learning from a Pandemic to Prepare for the Future

Steven Shorrock

Abstract This chapter starts with the premise that the future of work is unpredictable. This has been illustrated by the COVID-19 pandemic, and further profound changes in contexts of work will bring significant and volatile changes to future work, as well as health, safety, security, and productivity. Micronarrative testimony from healthcare practitioners whose work has been affected dramatically by the emergence of the pandemic is used in this chapter to derive learning from experience of this major change. The narratives concern the nature of responding to a rapidly changing world, work-as-imagined and work-as-done, human-centred design and systems thinking and practice, and leadership and social capital. Seven learning points were drawn from clinicians' reflections that may be more widely relevant to the future of work.

Keywords Health care · COVID-19 · Change · Work-as-imagined · Work-as-done · Work-as-prescribed · Adaptation

12.1 Introduction

The future of work is, self-evidently, unknown to us. The future of work has become what is now popularly known as "work-as-imagined" [5]. While this term is often used to describe imagined work now or in the past, it equally applies to work in future. Experience shows that our imagination of the past and present is incomplete and incorrect in fundamental ways. And so, of course, our imagination of the future is even more limited. It is unpredictable, in that it is not possible reliably to characterise with confidence—except in some very broad terms—the details and patterns in the nature of work in the coming decades.

This presents a dilemma for a writer looking to envisage the future of work in a few years, let alone in 2030, and beyond. At the time of writing, the COVID-19 pandemic has changed work dramatically within one year in almost all sectors of industry, and is living demonstration of the limits of imagination applied to the future

---

S. Shorrock (✉)
EUROCONTROL, Brétigny sur Orge, France
e-mail: steven.shorrock@eurocontrol.int

of work. Research projects and white papers in health care and aviation, for instance, on the future of work have lost some relevance with fundamental changes to the nature of work brought about by COVID-19.

What we *can* reliably predict about the future of work is that it will change unpredictably and significantly. Changes are likely to involve many "aspects of context": geopolitical, political, legal, regulatory, judicial, economic, societal, social, cultural, environmental, organisational, technological, and informational, with implications for health, safety, security, productivity, and work in general. The changes will require adaptations at all levels of the system, from front-line staff and service users to regulators and governments. The pandemic has therefore offered an opportunity to look at how work has changed in the light of significant unforeseen events, and how workers and organisations have responded, in the hope of drawing some lessons that may remain valid in the coming decades.

In this chapter, I take a narrative approach to understanding aspects of the future of work, relying not primarily on the predictions and reflections of previous authors, or my own, but the high-context accounts of front-line healthcare workers, whose work has been affected dramatically by the emergence of the pandemic. Using a rapid, micronarrative research approach [7], combining aspects of narrative inquiry and grounded theory [6], I aimed to explore and conceptualise clinicians' experience in textual form. Via twitter, I asked known healthcare practitioners to answer the following question: *What have you learned about work from the COVID-19 pandemic?* I requested that answers be limited to around 100 words. The reason for this was to allay expectations of a long, written response (which deter response, especially among busy healthcare professionals) and to encourage respondents to prioritise the most important learning points for them, via reflection-on-action [9].

The data from the 24 participants were subject to thematic analysis and are presented in this chapter with associated learning points, providing insights into front-line experiences of work that may apply to other workers in health care, and beyond.

12.2 Responding to a Rapidly Changing World

In the light of the likelihood of future disruptions (e.g. pandemics, major outages, climate change), the COVID-19 pandemic has illustrated how the future of work will involve responding to volatility and unpredictability, requiring timely adaption. The importance of front-line involvement in such change was emphasised by several clinicians. That "people are the solution" was noted in the context of many healthcare functions. Participant 1 (Intensivist, Australia) stated that the only thing we can reliably predict about the future is the need for change, and that "Frontline workers are the solution to most problems that will inevitably arise. They are the most valuable resource in healthcare, both for delivering the care and for designing how to do it". His remark mirrors contemporary thinking about safety. As Cook [2] noted,

> Human practitioners are the adaptable element of complex systems

and

> The system continues to function because it contains so many redundancies and because people can make it function, despite the presence of many flaws.

Dekker [3] (p. vi) sees

> people as the source of diversity, insight, creativity, and wisdom about safety, not as sources of risk that undermine an otherwise safe system.

The need for rapid response was mentioned by several clinicians. Some noted the need for interdisciplinary collaboration on a scale never seen previously. A specific example was provided by Participant 2 (Anaesthetist and Health Education England Simulation Lead, England) in the context of the new major "Nightingale" hospital in the UK, where he "witnessed enormous willingness and motivation amongst practitioners and managers to respond to the need for rapid change". Reflecting on prior inertia in health care, he noted that "This felt like a big contrast from previous 'norms' of organisational behaviour in healthcare". Similarly, in an ambulance context, Participant 3 (Ambulance Service Patient Safety Manager, Scotland) discovered that "some types of ambulance service work systems that would previously have been considered very difficult to change, can actually be reconfigured at pace and new ways of working can be introduced, which lead to significantly different system performance". Participant 4 (Anaesthetist, Australia) noted also how health care has "a reputation for resistance to change".

While many workers, especially those in office-based roles, have switched to working from home with extensive use of videoconferencing, a corresponding change in health care has been a switch to telemedicine. Participant 5 (Emergency Physician, USA) described how the job changed rapidly from in-person clinical care: "Our telemedicine urgent care started seeing hundreds of COVID patients a day, a disease and volume that were totally new to us". This clinician, and her colleagues, learned to adapt rapidly to the new conditions, which presented challenging trade-offs.

Self-organisation and staff-developed standard operating procedures (SOPs) extended to other hospital functions. Participant 6 (Radiologist, England) noted that homeworking was arranged rapidly "after years of dragging feet". This was helped by having the required IT equipment already available, but not set up, in hospital, as well as adaptive IT support. "Radiologists were split into two groups", he wrote, "one at home, one in department. Radiographers worked out their own rotas. Radiographers and nursing staff worked on SOPs for imaging COVID positive patients".

Some indicated, however, that the degree of clinician involvement in change was variable, with a contrast between top-down change done "to" people and change done "with" and "by" people [as discussed by Russell [8], in terms of "modes of change"]. Participant 4 (Anaesthetist, Australia) highlighted especially the "to" mode of change—top-down initiated change, with limited clinician consultation, particularly regarding the rationing of personal protective equipment (PPE). Other organisations, she wrote, have initiated clinician-led processes, "resulting in durable models of care but uncovering 'wicked problems'". Participant 4 reflected, "COVID-19 has taught me that engaging clinicians doing the work increases short-term complexity, but doing otherwise risks failure in the long term, losing trust on the way". This can be seen as an acute-chronic trade-off [4] in responding to change.

Participant 7 (Intensivist, New Zealand) noted the importance of diverse views for solving complex, dynamic problems, such as the rapid reconfiguration of an intensive care unit (ICU). "This required many different teams: ICU clinicians, infection control nurses, biomedical engineers, builders, ventilation engineers and quality improvement specialists". This clinician highlighted the importance of pre-existing relationships, in this case built up during a prior volcanic burns incident.

Similarly, in a French ICU context, Participant 8 (Anesthesiologist, France) wrote of the need for more ICU beds. "Equipment wasn't designed for ICU, nor were newly formed teams used to working together in this stressful environment". He noted the effectiveness of "collective intelligence via inclusive collaboration and open communication" for preventing harm both to patients and to healthcare workers.

An iterative approach to adaptation to keep pace with a rapidly evolving situation, especially in the context of uncertain and volatile information, was the focus of Participant 9 (Intensivist, New Zealand): "By starting to address problems iteratively we could create a network of actions that we could knit together. We rapidly developed a tolerance of failures, using them, with active feedback, to modify our processes and facilities adaptively, alongside the new information that became available".

The requirement for rapid responses is sometimes confounded by the economic and organisational contexts, including resource constraints, communication channels, and the political context, such as policy and communication. Participant 2 noted his experience of challenges to redesigning clinical services in the context of constraints such as "workforce availability, skill mix and preparedness for redeployment; creating and adapting new clinical environments; accessing critical specialised equipment and supplies quickly and reliably". Similarly, Participant 10 (Professor of Health care, England) highlighted "the structural and cultural barriers to leveraging talent in surge demand". Characterising the limitations of blunt-end response to changes in work, she noted that "It's like a slow-moving major incident without the implementation of a major incident plan".

12.3 Work-as-Imagined and Work-as-Done

Several respondents highlighted differences between work-as-imagined and work-as-done (WAI-WAD), concepts that have recently gained currency in health care. Participant 11 (Surgeon, Scotland) stated that the pandemic "has shone a light on how we work, and the dichotomy between 'work-as-imagined and work-as-done'". Participant 4 reflected that "It is critical that 'work-as-prescribed' reflects 'work-as-done' to prevent depletion of the workforce through infection and exhaustion". A specific example mentioned by some respondents was PPE. Participant 12 (Anaesthetist, England) noted that, despite 25 years working in anaesthesia, the COVID-19 pandemic presented his first introduction to PPE and FFP3 masks. Fit testing and training in PPE donning and doffing was, however, not adequate preparation for the daily challenges of working in PPE. "The impact of heat, the need for good hydration, and the communication challenges became stressors—recognised and managed by great team working through adaptations in how we worked". He remarked further that, "Looking back, local practice is not 'work-as-prescribed'".

Participant 13 (Consultant Anaesthetist, England) also commented on unimagined and unintended consequences of PPE: "Working in PPE is hot, tiring and difficult to both hear and see. Staff avoid drinking to reduce bathroom visits, all of which affects their ability to work. Extra time is taken from patient care to put on and take off the PPE". She noted that measures to reduce the risk of COVID indirectly affected patient safety in other unimagined ways. Participant 14 (Consultant in Emergency and Retrieval Medicine, Scotland) similarly reflected on unforeseen communication difficulties while wearing PPE, especially for aerosol-generating procedures. "Voices are muffled, hearing is compromised and implicit communication through facial expression is lost". He noted that this is a particular problem for resuscitation teams working under pressure.

Difficulties in compliance with work-as-prescribed [10] were noted by other respondents. Participant 15 (Former Critical Care Outreach Nurse, England) stated that some rules and guidance were developed by people remote from the work and were no longer applicable. "These rules end up being a barrier to do the right thing. For example, filling a 35-page safety booklet about a newly admitted patient takes us away from practical tasks such as personal care or administering medication".

Participant 15 stated that "Now, no-one knew the best way to do things. There was no evidence base to draw from, and no exemplars to follow". Participant 2 similarly noted policy-level problems: "multiple channels and frequent shifts in emphasis of central guidance and policy". This was reiterated by Participant 16 (Critical Care Nurse, South Africa), who cited "information overload, inconsistent messages and departure from plain common sense".

For Participant 15, the absence of written authority required a collaborative local approach. "Everyone came up with ideas, and many more came from social media", she wrote. "We openly learned from each other. We were finding solutions from the ground up and the senior leadership team listened".

The dearth of appropriate procedures and guidance was also noted by Participant 13: "Without timely clear guidance arriving down the traditional lines, the ability of staff to innovate and adapt was remarkable. The constraint of normal change bureaucracy was temporarily suspended and essential new ways of working arrived in a rapid and remarkably effective way, significantly prior to written SOPs". She stated that front-line staff instead required underlying principles [1] and developed and translated them in appropriate ways for their own local work and working environment. This leveraged the competency and expertise of military nurses who had significant experience with PPE and Ebola.

Team approaches to learning are needed to maximise the impact and ensure the safety of such adaptations, remarked Participant 17 (General Practitioner, Scotland): "In my GP practice, daily 'huddles' (short meetings) were used to discuss how we implemented rapidly changing guidance while coping with varying conditions (e.g. demand and capacity) and competing goals (e.g. reducing hospital admissions while maintaining patient safety)". These huddles encouraged sharing of innovative practice and increased understanding the rationale for decisions, and how decisions affected other parts of the system. They also "supported those making difficult decisions and ensured people did not drift into unsafe practices". Participant 11 (Surgeon, Scotland) also referred to an approach to team learning in Scotland involving regular reviews of reports by clinicians for the purpose of collective learning, which has helped to bridge this WAI-WAD gap.

Participant 14 (Consultant in Emergency and Retrieval Medicine, Scotland) and colleagues co-designed a checklist to improve communication using PPE called "PRESS": P—Pre-transmission pause. Think before you speak; R—Read back—close the loop; E—Eye contact—ensure focused attention; S—Say again—repeat critical information; and S—Shared team mental model with a team rally point.

Participant 13 (Consultant Anaesthetist, England) remarked that the WAI-WAD gap also applied to clinicians' imagination of "patient work": "Initially we asked our patients to self-isolate for 14 days prior to elective surgery, and (as we knew the reasons) we imagined that they would do that unquestioningly. We 'prescribed' that to them, without explanation, and then anyone who proceeded to surgery had to 'disclose' that they had completed this. Only the patient ever knew whether they had done so". She stated that it took time to identify this gap, which is taking longer still to close.

Participant 3 (Ambulance Service Patient Safety Manager, Scotland) noted that the WAI-WAD gap can be minimal for changes up to a certain scale. However, "with larger groups of workforce, it can be very difficult to influence multiple, often subtle, changes in work-as-done to match with the more easily changeable work-as-prescribed (and work-as-imagined)". He noted that this was particularly evident in the early stages of the response phase when clinical, logistical and PPE criteria were becoming established.

A word of warning was sounded by Participant 18 (Anaesthesiologist, USA), about rapidly created bottom-up methods. "Although this pandemic has brought lots of new concepts and working conditions, it's imperative that we maintain our usual high standards and not be tempted to try new techniques and alter our usual routine safe practice". Participant 7 usefully expanded that, in the New Zealand intensive care context "the redesign of clinical work was based on four requirements: to be SAFE, SIMPLE, SUSTAINABLE and ADAPTABLE". Reflecting more recent focus in safety management on everyday work, he noted that "the ability to anticipate potential challenges required imagination and a deep understanding of the realities of everyday work".

Participant 19 (Anesthesiologist-Intensivist, France) noted the role of acceptance of uncertainty, and humility: "This whole experience was new for everyone. For many professionals, it has created a touching sense of humility, both among frontline actors and managers. I believe that this humility has facilitated communication and the emergence of a shared governance between caregivers and administrators where

I've been working". He noted that, for the first time, work and its goals were shared and the WAI-WAD gap was minimal.

12.4 Human-Centred Design and Systems Thinking and Practice

Adaptive imagination is necessary to respond tactically, or even opportunistically, to rapidly changing circumstances, but there remains a need for more strategic human-centred design and systems thinking in design, and therefore a need for support to integrate appropriate approaches. Traditionally, such approaches are seen as more "blunt end" analysis and support (often over the timescale of months or years), but there is a need for more rapid integration into operations (over the timescale of days or weeks). There is therefore a requirement to balance the need for rapid, user-led change with durable user-centred design.

Emergency care is an aspect of health care characterised by improvisation. Participant 20 (Emergency Physician, Trauma Team Leader and Simulation Educator, Canada) reflected on the nature of emergency care. "Healthcare is a precarious thing, balancing on the backs individual and team resourcefulness and resilience. Emergency medicine, in particular, suffers from 'ad hoc-itis'. Our ability to improvise solutions in the face of massive systemic limitations and inefficiencies is practically a professional badge of honour". Participant 20 stated that COVID-19 has highlighted the need for more understanding of complex system design. "We can build systems that make sense. We can use simulation-informed design, prototype testing, multi-source feedback and hazard analysis to help manage complexity rather than compel us to work against it". He remarked that the pandemic requires a rethink of how health services adapt, beyond front-line tactical or opportunistic adaptations: "and therein lies a massive challenge and unprecedented opportunity: let user-centred and data-driven design lead us in rebuilding".

Participant 1 (Intensivist, Australia) remarked there has been some success with this. "Locally, we have seen rapid, successful innovation of work practices through the marriage of simulation and human-centred design principles".

Human-centred design does, however, need to be embedded in systems practice. One of the fundamental activities of systems thinking involves making boundary judgements. Participant 21 (Anaesthetist, Scotland) stated that "Where you draw the system boundary matters. I started chairing a theatre COVID preparedness group in March. We quickly transformed the theatre complex to handle a surge in patients with COVID, while keeping staff safe. We liaised with ED, ICU and the wards which are upstream/downstream of theatres". The teamwork, dynamism, and psychological safety of the working group, he said, were critical. The system boundary chosen did not include the whole hospital system, since others were focusing on this. However, there were other aspects of the health and social care system that would have benefitted from the group's input: "Looking back now I wonder about the care homes.

They were not within my system and I didn't give them a second's thought within my planning. Whose system boundary included care homes? What were their working conditions, demands and constraints?"

12.5 Leadership and Social Capital

In the narratives above, the importance of teamwork has been emphasised. More generally, clinicians remarks concerned leadership, human relations, and social capital. Participant 19 (Anesthesiologist-Intensivist, France) stated that "COVID appears to have acted as a powerful inductor for team building". He found that "strongly empathetic and benevolent leadership can have a positive impact on patient safety, work organisation, coping and caregivers' well-being". Participant 22 (Midwife, England) similarly noted that "The need for sincerity and genuine characteristics is essential. A focus on leadership over management is required. Midwifery managers/consultants need to be able to utilise the clinical skills they started off with to enable support and understanding of their units in today's world".

Participant 18 (Anaesthesiologist, USA) noted the need to "foster good relational coordination amongst colleagues particularly during a time of great uncertainty and constant change". Participant 23 (Anaesthetist, Australia) similarly highlighted the criticality of high-trust relationships to safety. Referring to the importance of bridging social capital, she noted how "The pandemic has required groups to leave their silos and to collaborate rapidly on high-stakes issues". Some professionals (Participant 19 noted specifically aerodynamic scientists and occupational hygienists) had not previously routinely been included in healthcare teams to keep workers and patients safe. With a nod to the technological context of work, she also mentioned that "many of these experts are accessible on social media, primarily twitter, and have been generously sharing their expertise for the benefit of all". This rapid, interprofessional adaptation—outside of organisational boundaries—arguably could not have happened without social media.

Participant 15 (Critical Care Outreach Nurse, England) stated that the "flattened hierarchy" does not imply effective leadership, but can be a barrier to effective communication. "For example, everyone is wearing the same outfits, no name badges are shown and no one recognises anyone. So who is the leader? Being involved in a medical emergency with no leadership evident is a scary place to be". According to Participant 15, the role of a decisive leader has been critical during the pandemic: "[It] has given me comfort and guidance when I have felt as if I was floundering".

Participant 24 (Orthopaedic Resident, Poland) remarked that "During the pandemic, I learned that no matter how well organised the healthcare system is, you end up counting on good people to do everything they can to overcome and minimise effects of hopefully rare but inevitable system flaws".

12.6 Lessons for Future Work

From the micronarratives collected, a number of lessons can be drawn for future work, whether in the coming years or decades. While the context will change, many of the lessons that can be identified from these narratives would appear to be relevant. I have drawn the following lessons from the narratives:

1. resistance to change within organisations can ease rapidly in the face of major disruptions to normal work;
2. leveraging the expertise of staff in their own work will be key to responding to change. Involvement of diverse perspectives, especially those of front-line staff, is necessary for short- and long-term adaptation to change;
3. pre-existing relationships and investment in bonding and bridging social capital are required for adaptive response at scale;
4. complicated procedures designed to ensure thoroughness may become a barrier to effectiveness, resulting in abandonment. Procedures and policies should therefore be backed up by principles or a more general philosophy;
5. adapting to change requires sufficient resources (relating to people, equipment, supplies, infrastructure), which must be planned and made available in advance;
6. iterative cycles of understanding and intervention, at micro-, meso-, and macro-system levels, are important for adaptation, and approaches to tactical risk management and improvement should be taught to staff. Human-centred design, and tactical adaptations to work, needs to be embedded in systems thinking and practice, which should be part of general education and development;
7. differences between work-as-imagined and work-as-done exist between all stakeholder groups need to be understood via regular discussions and reviews of everyday work practices and specific events.

Ethical Statement Data collection and reporting is undertaken under a protocol that informs participants of the use of their testimonies, with anonymisation of interviewees and health facilities.

References

1. I. Barshi, A. Degani, R. Mauro, L. Loukopoulou, Guiding the practice: the 4 P's. Hindsight **25**, 50–53 (2017)
2. R.I. Cook, How complex systems fail. HindSight **31**, 13–16 (2020)
3. S. Dekker, *Safety Differently: Human Factors for a New Era*, 2nd edn. (CRC Press, 2015)

4. R.R. Hoffman, D.D. Woods, Beyond Simon's slice: five fundamental trade-offs that bound the performance of macrocognitive work systems. IEEE Intell. Syst. **26**(6) (2011). https://doi.org/10.1109/MIS.2011.97
5. E. Hollnagel, Can we ever imagine how work is done? Hindsight **25**, 10–13 (2017)
6. S. Lal, M. Suto, M. Ungar, Examining the potential of combining the methods of grounded theory and narrative inquiry: a comparative analysis. Qual. Rep. **17**, 1–22 (2012). Retrieved from http://www.nova.edu/ssss/QR/QR17/lal.pdf
7. Patient Safety Translational Research Centre, Micronarratives—staff micronarratives as a source of soft intelligence on safety (2021). Retrieved from https://yhpstrc.org/research-themes-partners/digital-innovations-for-patient-safety/our-projects/micronarratives-use-of-staff-reported-micronarratives-as-a-source-of-real-time-soft-intelligence-on-patient-safety/
8. C. Russell, Four modes of change: to, for, with, by. Hindsight **28**, 8–11 (2019)
9. D.A. Schön, *The Reflective Practitioner: How Professionals Think in Action* (Routledge, 1983)
10. S. Shorrock, *The Varieties of Human Work* (2016). Retrieved from Humanistic systems: https://humanisticsystems.com/2016/12/05/the-varieties-of-human-work/

Open Access This chapter is licensed under the terms of the Creative Commons Attribution 4.0 International License (http://creativecommons.org/licenses/by/4.0/), which permits use, sharing, adaptation, distribution and reproduction in any medium or format, as long as you give appropriate credit to the original author(s) and the source, provide a link to the Creative Commons license and indicate if changes were made.

The images or other third party material in this chapter are included in the chapter's Creative Commons license, unless indicated otherwise in a credit line to the material. If material is not included in the chapter's Creative Commons license and your intended use is not permitted by statutory regulation or exceeds the permitted use, you will need to obtain permission directly from the copyright holder.

Chapter 13
Conjectures and Challenges of Safety Management

A Peek at the Future

Jean Pariès

Abstract Climate disruption, changing demographics, globalisation, financialisation, industrial and economic fragmentation and complexification, mass digitalisation are all major changes currently taking place in the world and in societies, and theoretically, they will accelerate by 2030–2040. The impact of these major trends on the strategies for managing industrial safety is a rather underexplored topic that is the subject of this collaborative book. This final chapter looks at some of the lessons from the book and places them in perspective by offering conjectures on the place of the human operator, the responsibility of stakeholders and organisations, the reliability and vulnerability of sociotechnical systems, the strategic vision of safety… Taking into account this range of possibilities and the challenges the industrial sector is facing, it proposes avenues to explore so that, in future, risks continue to be managed to the standards expected by society.

Keywords Human reliability · Responsibility · Safety strategy · Anticipation · Complexity · Instability · Adaptation · Politics

13.1 Changes in the World and Changes in the Minds

Like many others, this book starts from the premise that the world is undergoing a radical, global change, and on the scale of the history of societies, this is occurring at an extremely fast pace. In fact, everything is changing. The long-announced global warming is confirming its inexorable nature and beginning to show the power it has to destabilise habitats, the economy, ways of life and relationships to the environment. The world population will continue to grow exponentially for decades, particularly in Africa, and stagnate and age considerably in the most economically developed regions. It will inevitably redistribute itself through mass migrations. The value production chain continues to be relocated offshore to countries with cheap labour.

J. Pariès (✉)
FonCSI-ICSI, Toulouse, France
e-mail: jean.paries@foncsi.icsi-eu.org

© The Author(s) 2022
H. Laroche et al. (eds.), *Managing Future Challenges for Safety*,
SpringerBriefs in Safety Management,
https://doi.org/10.1007/978-3-031-07805-7_13

Its organisations are becoming globalised, financialised, fragmented and complexified in increasingly interdependent networks. Galloping digitalisation, virtualisation, machine/deep learning, along with mass connectivity and data processing are transforming attitudes towards the company, production and work. The financial stakes take such a high priority and are so huge that, for the 737 Max, the top management of Boeing imposed on its legendary engineering team technical choices that defied common sense and the basic rules of design. The Big Five are becoming the leaders of the global economy. Their stock market value far exceeds the GDP of France. That of Tesla has reached the trillion-dollar mark, making its value one hundred times higher than that of Renault and higher than all of the other car manufacturers in the world combined. Elon has become a popular first name.

The list does not end there, and the deeper meaning of these transformations is a source of debate. But while the trajectory is not yet clear, one thing is certain: the scale and momentum of the changes underway are those of the major 'revolutions' in history. In other words, this is a metamorphosis of society. Based on this observation, this book poses the question: "What will be the impact of this metamorphosis on industrial risk management strategies and, more precisely, on the place of human actors in these strategies?" And incidentally: "What would need to be done, today or tomorrow, so that in the future the industrial sector continues to manage its risks to the standards expected by society?"

These questions are difficult for two reasons. Because prediction is a difficult art, particularly in a period of radical changes. But also, because the very notion of safety strategy remains unclear, or even contradictory in some respects. The introduction to this book highlighted this by putting in perspective the official safety model, based on predetermination and total control, and a practical model which more realistically integrates uncertainties and necessary adaptations. And the 'objective' world is not the only one changing. Our mental representations of it are also changing, as the real world remains constant. The models are changing; the theories themselves are undergoing major 'revolutions'. And in this dual process, the changes in 'reality' and changes in 'theory' interfere with one another. As seen with COVID-19, certain unshakeable certainties regarding 'budgetary orthodoxy' or the benefits of globalisation were… shaken. What was 'impossible' became necessary. Conversely, this blow to the theory will also generate or facilitate changes to the economic 'reality' post-COVID-19.

The same is true in the field of safety. More particularly, as regards the place of the human operator in safety, industrial views and practices have changed a great deal over the last three decades. The integration of knowledge from the human sciences into the safety model has profoundly transformed it. The view of the operator and of 'human reliability' has changed. The initial equation (safety = technical reliability + obedient operator) has become more complex. The operator has become a 'fallible reliability agent' in an environment that is itself recognised as less predictable, requiring some adaptations in real time. And thus, an 'intelligently obedient' operator, and more open, cooperative leaders who are willing to listen.

13.2 The Future of the 'Compliant yet Intelligent Operator' Injunction

One could conjecture that this model will be little affected by the transformations underway. We already know most of the processes at work: automation, virtualisation of activities by putting distance between the human operator and the real-time physical process, replacement of the human operator with robots, transformation of the actor into a supervisor. These changes have occurred in several industries, notably in aviation. They will spread to other industries and, within each of these, to more occupations higher up in the pecking order (e.g. doctors rather than nurses). This will mobilise new, more disruptive technologies and will involve human–machine interactions complexified by artificial intelligence (AI) and machine learning. Overall, the remaining operators will find it even more difficult to construct a 'mental model' of the machine and to predict and understand what it is doing. We already know the associated negative effects: overconfidence in the machine; loss of comprehension; issues with alertness; loss of basic know-how, which remains crucial in degraded mode. We also know that they can be partly controlled and that the final outcome is most often favourable or even highly favourable to safety.

The most reasonable conjecture is thus that the number of safety issues associated with the reliability of frontline operators will continue to drop significantly when it comes to designed-for and normal operation. One corollary is that the onus should shift from the users of the systems to their designers unless, like Tesla and their colleagues, these designers manage to convince everyone that the operators are always 'in charge' of said systems. However, the capacity of operators to intervene and take over control in 'beyond design basis' situations will also diminish drastically. And it will become less and less possible for operators to offset this tendency with a better knowledge of the systems they are handling, as these will have become too complex and inexorably 'esoteric' in degraded mode. Should we still feel the need to maintain some level of control over 'beyond design basis' situations, the 'sense-making' ability of the operational team will need to be improved by giving them real-time access to the necessary network of expertise, and the systems will have to be designed to include a mode of operation which does not require access to causality, similar to the 'state-based control' used in the nuclear plants when proper understanding is lost, in contrast with event-based control. This will imply training the designers in complexity, its consequences and its management, a great deal more than they are right now.

But at the level of the organisation, the company, and even more so at the level of society as a whole (public, media, justice political arena), the safety strategy is still largely perceived as resulting from the capacity to anticipate all situations, to predetermine the right technical and human solutions and to ensure conformity with what was anticipated. All of this through an increasingly detailed formalisation, a 'rationalisation' of the system, processes and activities, and through ensuring their quality ("we write down what we do, we do what is written, and this is what protects us against lawsuits if an accident does occur"). In short, a model of a programmed, deterministic and linear machine, controlled by an all-powerful 'command and control' system, which knows nothing of 'beyond design basis'.

13.3   Rise and Fall of a Paradigm Shift

Yet, for the past three decades at least, some scientific schools of thought[1] have proposed other visions of safety, built on the recognition of the dynamic complexity of the sociotechnical systems that constitute the industrial world. This 'complexity' means constant and irreducible variability, turbulence, circular causality, nonlinearity between the causes and the effects, interference, resonance, long-range coupling, 'butterfly effect', etc. In that world, variation is part of the normal state and is the irreducible background noise to the 'life' of the system. The underlying metaphor is no longer that of a programmed machine, but that of a living system. Its survival does not imply the absence of deviations (on the contrary, these are an integral part of its evolution), but rather managing these, constantly compensating for them, blocking those that are unfavourable and selecting those that are favourable to adaptation and adaptability. And in this vision, safety is inseparable from the other vital objectives: it is not possible to get food or water without exposing oneself to predators. Resilience can only be thought of in terms of compromise between the different survival needs.

Unlike HOF, this systemic vision was not 'bought' by industrial safety. At least, not in its entirety. Though it is possible to identify certain aspects that have been partially borrowed. The COVID-19 crisis has trivialised the word "resilience" and sharpened our awareness that the only certainty is uncertainty, i.e. that unexpected and unpredictable things will happen. But as already mentioned, the safety 'paradigm' remains essentially tied to anticipation and predetermination. One could even say that it is becoming reinforced, with an increase in standards and compliance efforts. Incidentally, these are largely validated by the undeniable, and at times considerable, progress achieved in safety over the last decades. And today, a majority of the designers and strategists in the industrial sector are awaiting a new breakthrough in this strategy, thanks to the spectacular advances made in digitalisation, AI, big data, digital twins and deep learning, which they believe should bring a leap forward in modelling, prediction and monitoring capacities.

Yet, the analyses reported in this book clearly indicate that the current sociotechnological revolution will generate intense stress characteristic of great societal transformations and the adaptability challenges they bring. Europe will probably experience a strong shortage of specialised skills due to a gap between those produced by its universities and the needs of its industrial sector. The ageing of its workforce will be at odds with the need to have several successive occupations over the span of

---

[1] E.g., Normal Accident Theory (C. Perrow); High Reliability Organizations (T. Laporte & al.); Risk Management in a Dynamic Society (J. Rasmussen); Systems Theoretic Hazard Analysis Technique (N. Leveson); Resilience Engineering (D. Woods, E. Hollnagel & al.).

a career. Its cultural conversion, increasingly in favour of respecting the environment and living more frugally or even ascetically, will undoubtedly not catch on in the rest of the world, at least not initially. It risks a consecutive transfer of the nerve centres of its industries—design, normalisation, financing—to Asia, thus prolonging the migration of the value production chains. With the fragmentation and globalisation of the industrial sector, the technological innovations underway and those to come will surpass the monitoring and certification capacity of regulatory bodies to guarantee safety, as already illustrated by the challenges in certifying self-learning systems. The divide will widen between those (designers, major players) who will understand the algorithms and have access to the data and those who will 'consume' without understanding. Self-regulation and third parties (insurers, standards bodies, professional alliances) will increasingly replace official authorities. Systemic computer network failures and cybersecurity will replace operator reliability as the central concern for 'safety'. With the loss of intelligibility and the growing dissociation between benefit and risk, the risk aversion of the public, the users and local residents will continue to grow, and along with it distrust and suspicion, amplified by social media, in a world that is increasingly esoteric or even magical and has shifted into 'emergency' mode, destabilised by climate change and the boomerang effects of ecosystem destruction. More and more risks will become uninsurable.

Beyond this forecast, which will inevitably prove to be wrong and which, it is hoped, presents a pessimistic view, the socio-technological revolution underway could thus generate a real paradox. By extending the industrial fabric to a global scale while fragmenting it and multiplying the interconnections, the revolution inexorably increases its complexity and thus, by definition, the limits to its modelling, and the uncertainty and 'fundamental surprise' potential associated with it. At the same time, there is a growing feeling that the computing power is developing faster than the object of the modelling: since a future which can be entirely pre-calculated is now within reach with the digital twins, exhaustive predetermination and total control could be just around the corner. And there might finally be some kind of an end to safety risk management. In this, there is no doubt an illusion of the same nature as that which, at the end of the last century, believed the end of history was coming. This does not mean that all the promises of digital technology are false. It is certain that we will have factories, trains, aircraft and nuclear reactors controlled at levels one order of magnitude higher than our current best levels. But—this is a banality—this control will never be total. And most importantly, it will concern local processes, not the entire system. Accidents will become rarer, but increasingly of the 'black swan' type.

13.4 The Risk of a Late and Stale Evolution of Safety Management

Thus, everything is happening as though the story of safety was that of a slow ascension within the levels of the organisation, beginning with the machine, the operator and their workstation, continuing at the level of the teams, the workshops, the procedures, then the processes, the departments, the production sites. But, everything is also happening as though the safety strategy was always one level behind. The more complex the system becomes, the more the root factors, which 'produce' the risk and allow its modulation, shift to the next level up. We think about the workstation level when it is already the design and processes that are the issue, about the process level when it is already the company's strategy that is the issue and about the strategic decision-making level of a company when it is the global value production chain that is generating instabilities... And while safety studies are carried out for internal and local changes within the company, this is not the case for major changes affecting the world. Safety is leaving the confines of the company, and its systemic dimension is not being dealt with at the right level. If we are not careful, the future of safety will resemble that of antibiotics. Given our sterilisation strategies, the threat of the future is not so much the original pathogen, but the fact that our defences are always one mutation behind.

Therefore, it is important to get out of safety-focused circles to talk about safety. The challenges to safety lie elsewhere, in places little penetrated by safety. One of the findings of the 'Strategic Analysis[2]' that underpins this book is that the major changes in the world are questioned by researchers and specialists from a variety of fields, examined from numerous angles, but not from the safety angle, at least not as a priority. Safety appears as an orphan dimension of the reflexion. The major climatic, environmental, economic and geopolitical challenges are also discussed in influential circles, in think-tanks gathering world leaders, at the COP, Davos and the like. Conversely, although systemic safety now extends beyond the traditional places of discussion, which are the company and its interactions with public requirements via regulatory bodies, there are few if any places where they are discussed. There are few if any publications, meetings, organisations that discuss the impact of the major changes on safety.

Within companies, those in charge continue to think in terms of industrial safety associated with the 'internal' state of the company, even though the boundaries of the latter have burst. Thus, since major changes are played out in circles where safety is not a topic that is discussed, the challenge is to raise safety issues in these places of influence, create new places of influence where they will be discussed and reinforce the few that exist. This will not be easy. The topics are dictated by the scale and urgency of the issues. It is said that Stalin responded to Pierre Laval, then French Prime Minister visiting Moscow, who asked him to make a favourable

---

[2] Research methodology developed by FonCSI that brings together international academics and practitioners for inquiry and debate, and aims at providing FonCSI's partners with high-level results within 18–24 months.

gesture towards the Vatican: "The Pope? How many divisions?" Our strategists will ask: "Safety? How many billions?" Compared to the consequences of pandemics, global warming, increased extreme weather events and cyberattacks, it will not be much. With more and more focus on a few rare black swans, it may sound even less loud through the megaphone of social media. Safety experts are going to have to take serious lessons in mass influence and lobbying. In other words, in politics.

Open Access This chapter is licensed under the terms of the Creative Commons Attribution 4.0 International License (http://creativecommons.org/licenses/by/4.0/), which permits use, sharing, adaptation, distribution and reproduction in any medium or format, as long as you give appropriate credit to the original author(s) and the source, provide a link to the Creative Commons license and indicate if changes were made.

The images or other third party material in this chapter are included in the chapter's Creative Commons license, unless indicated otherwise in a credit line to the material. If material is not included in the chapter's Creative Commons license and your intended use is not permitted by statutory regulation or exceeds the permitted use, you will need to obtain permission directly from the copyright holder.

The manufacturer's authorised representative in the EU is Springer Nature Customer Service Centre GmbH, Europaplatz 3, 69115 Heidelberg, Germany. If you have any concerns regarding our products, please contact ProductSafety@springernature.com

Printed and bound by CPI Group (UK) Ltd, Croydon, CR0 4YY

25/03/2026

02078170-0010